The Choice is Yours

YOU ARE NOT DEFINED BY
YOUR CIRCUMSTANCES

COURTNEY GARDNER
&
JENNIFER GREGG

Sunflowers come in a number of varieties—ranging from small to very large, from having yellow petals to red. However, there is more to sunflowers than what meets the eye. While they are stunningly beautiful, they also are rich in history and meaning. Sunflowers symbolize adoration, loyalty, and longevity. Much of the meaning of sunflowers stems from its namesake, the sun itself. These flowers are unique in that they have the ability to provide energy in the form of nourishment and vibrancy—attributes which mirrors the sun and the energy provided by its heat and light (ProFlowers Blog, 2019).

Table of Contents

Acknowledgements

Courtney:

I would like to first acknowledge my grandmother, without her I would not be here, she is my strength, my rock, my everything.

Secondly, my sons, Boston you are heaven sent and I am immensely blessed and honored with being your mother. I have learned so much about myself, my strengths, and my abilities. More importantly you have taught me about life, how to enjoy the moments, how to appreciate the small things, and how to keep going. Wale, even though you are not here yet and you're still baking in the oven we are all excited to meet you!

To my gift children, Aaliyah, Elijah, and Nyaja I promise you it is the greatest gift to have you in my life. You have shown me that my heart can expand outside of myself. I love each of you as my own and I will forever be grateful for the trust you have instilled in me, thank you for allowing me to be your gift mother.

To April and Nate thank you for being the perfect parents for me, without you there is literally no me. You both are enough. I love you.

To mom Lyd you have left such a profound impact on my life. Thank you for taking me in and loving me as your own.

To my support system y'all know who y'all are! My sisters Aunie Nae and Auntie Mina y'all are the truest definitions of aunts, best friends, extended mothers, thank you for loving my children the way I love them. My brothers, Uncle Justin and Uncle Jules, I dont know how or why but y'all are always there at a drop of a dime, I love and appreciate you both. Essa, thanks for being the constant grandmother in Boston's life, "grandmothers matter". To my cousins, I love you, you each inspire me daily. I could not be all of what I am without you all. Thank you all for the support you have given me.

To my besties, Calina, Christine, & Lindar thank you all for challenging me, hearing me, and holding me accountable I love you all.

To Daniel thank you for gifting me with my children... thank you for the constant challenges, I have grown in many ways since you have been in my life.

To those who have taken a chance on me, and have trusted me as their coach, Thank You!

Jenn, my business bestie, it has been a wrap since we linked up, the world is in ours!

Lastly, but not least God and my ancestors (both known and unknown), thank you for your guidance, and continued support as I walk this earthly plan. Thank you for ears to hear, eyes to see, and a mind to think. I appreciate everything you have done for me, thank you, thank you, thank you.

Jennifer:

This book is dedicated to my loving Father, John H. Gregg, Jr. Thank you for every single seed you planted. I am grateful for the love and lessons you bestowed on me in this lifetime. I will continue to make you proud and will forever be a Daddy's girl. I miss your physical presence every day. Love always and forever, your Jenny Lukes.

To my Mother, Marie Elizabeth Dennis Gregg, thank you for being you. I am still so amazed how you moved from another country for love. That is so magical. I am grateful for everything especially your prayers. Also, I know with every phone call I will be guaranteed a laugh. Thank you for all the lessons in this life. I love you, forever.

To My baby sister, Kellye R. Gregg, when I think about our relationship, I get overwhelmed. I am so blessed to have a best friend, confidant, accountability partner, comedian, counselor, travel partner, and so much more in you. Please remember seasons will change and our roles will change but I will love you forever.

To my village (Aunts, Uncles, Cousins, Play Aunts/Uncles, God Parents, God Sisters and brothers, Sister-Cousins, Therapists, Life Coaches, Mentors, Spiritual Advisors, Teachers, BFFs, Close Girl and Guy friends, Family Friends, Trainers, Hair/Makeup Artists), thank you for being a part of my growth. I love and appreciate you all. I now fully understand what it means to say that it takes a village to raise a child.

To my ancestors known and unknown, thank you for paving a way. I am grateful for all your sacrifices. To my relatives that have gone on before me, I miss you. Thank you for watching over me.

To my close friends that have become family, thank you for being amazing. Thank you for understanding the busy spells in life. Thank you for the genuine love and support. I am so grateful for the bond we have created over the years. I love you.

To my God Children, you are the best. To the parents of my God Children, thank you for choosing me and trusting me with such an incredible honor. I love you all.

To my journey teachers (family, friends, co-workers, ex anything, acquaintances and anyone else I have crossed paths with), thank you for all the lessons in love and life.

To my current, future, and past clients, thank you for allowing and trusting me to pour into you. You have been a blessing in my life. Thank you for doing the work. Thank you for investing in yourself. I am so proud of you and excited for your next chapters in this life.

To my mentees, you are amazing. Thank you for allowing me to guide you. You are a blessing in my life and I know you all will do amazing things. I will be here cheering you on.

To my business besties, partners, vendors, accountants, people that I have collaborated with and anyone else that has contributed to the success of JGJI, thank you so very much. Let's continue to work and grow.

To my future husband and children, I am looking forward to sharing my future chapters of life with you. I have been putting in the work to be the best version of me for you. I love you so much, already.

To Donita, Tivern, Lezley, Baby Juju and Evonne, thank you for your time and energy. Thank you for your part in making this book's cosmetics pop! You are all so talented and we couldn't have done it without you.

Courtney, my darling, pinch me! We did it! Cheers!

To the person reading this right now, thank you for taking the time to purchase and read this book. Thank you for coming along for this ride with us. I pray that at least one thing in this book resonates with you.

CHAPTER 1

Introduction…. she slid into my DMs

⚜

T he universe never ceases to amaze me. A few years ago, while working on another event, one of my close girlfriends shared an idea as a suggestion for my next event. I thought it was a great idea and my initial thought was that I would like to partner up with a career coach, but did I know any? I jotted that note down, to come back to it later, and went on planning the upcoming event. Let me just say that when you are clear with your intentions, and in a ready position, the universe will deliver. No one knew about the note I made that day, except God. Within a week of that note, Courtney slid in my DMs. Wait! Let me backup a bit. For those that are not familiar with this term, DMs = Direct Messages. We live in an era of heavy social media and normally when you get a direct message (on any social media platform) it's unwarranted solicitation from someone trying to sell you something, some pyramid scheme, a romantic interest, or other annoying memos. I am not saying that *all* DMs are not important or should have a less than favorable connotation associated to them but just wanted to shed some quick light, for those that don't know, where the "sliding in my DMs" stems from. Now, that that is over with, let's get back to Courtney.

"Hey Jenn, I don't know if you know but I'm a life coach too (*specifically a success coach*). We should link up and partner on something ...tell me what you think!" I remember thinking hmmm, she seems nice but let me check her out. I went on Courtney's page, started looking at her posts, responded to the message she sent me....and then the sparks flew and the rest is history. We would later find out that we were both Aquarians-- birthdays are days apart from one another, born the same year-- and even though we were from different areas and walks of life, we shared similar stories of overcoming childhood trauma(s) to be the women we are today. In addition, we both love helping others become better versions of themselves. The first event we did was successful because not only do we work well together but we think and move the same. If one forgets something the other remembered and vice versa. It just works and I for one will say how grateful I am that the universe sought for us to cross paths.

When Courtney and I decided to write this book (another random conversation that we brought to fruition), we wanted to give people an intimate look into our journey; individually and collectively; where we came from, and where we are today. I love meeting and chatting with new people and it's always fascinating how strangers can have so much in common. The same is true for Courtney and I. Side bar: I often use self-disclosure when working with my clients because I feel like it helps build trust, which ultimately leads to a better client/coach relationship. With that being said, I went back and forth for a bit on using *full* disclosure with telling my story in this book. Why? Well, I don't mind sharing my story. Even the less than favorable parts all have played a role in making the woman I am today and the woman I continue to evolve into. The indecisive part is that there are so many parts of my story and of course there are several "characters" that played a role in my journey. I want to be respectful of their identities and privacy however I want to be as authentic as possible when telling my story. Obviously, I can't get over 30 years into these chapters, but my hope is that *my story* will inspire someone. When I say my story, I want everyone to keep in mind, this is how I coded the events of my life. With that being said, I do acknowledge and favor the well known saying *there are three sides to every story.*

I think everyone has *at least one* book inside of them. Why? Because everyone has a story. It has taken me way longer than I initially thought to write this book because of busy spells, life's happenings, and of course the negative self-talk with self-sabotage. How could I carry out my goal without having people look at my family a certain way? Where was this feeling stemming from? How can this be a bad thing when it was my story? My truth? My genuine desire was to help, heal, and inspire change? Sometimes my self-reflection is my arch nemesis. Like so many others, I was raised to keep family business, family business. That means you don't tell your parent's age, how much they make, what goes on behind closed doors, etc. I was taught to un-subconsciously suppress years and years and years of "stuff" by smiling when I was broken inside. I was dressing the part, showing up, going through the motions...until depression set in. I will touch more on this later. I always tell people you can't run from your stuff. No matter how long you think you can brush things under the rug, ignore it, move away, cover it with makeup, date someone new, have surgery, exercise/eat it away, it will catch up with you until you face it. By the way it's usually when you least expect it. Take it from me, someone who learned the hard way. Depression is nothing to play with and it has no prejudice of race, gender, or age. Oh, and it also shows up whenever it sees fit. As I said above, we will go more into this later on.

I am currently at peace with telling my story. I am doing this not to be malicious or "shame" any of my *journey teachers* that have contributed to making me into the woman I am today. A *Journey teacher* is anyone that you come across during your journey in life. These people include your parents, family members, siblings, children, friends, boyfriends, girlfriends, bosses, co-workers, etc. These teachers help mold you into the person you're intended to be. My hope is that my story will not only inspire someone but will help someone become a better version of themselves. I truly believe that everything happens for a reason and because I did my work and continue to do it, I am able to share my story. One of the many things I've learned along my journey is no one is perfect--no one is all good and no one is all bad. We are here for a short time and I want to inspire people to LIVE while they are here. I get this tiny pang of regret when I think of how much I have probably missed out on in the last few years because I was too "scared" to take a risk, or too shy to speak up, or too worried to be bold. It is my one wild and precious life, after all. In my professional opinion, you can start to *really* LIVE when you release the things that hold you down. You were born to fly but you can't take flight with heavy baggage...even airlines have restrictions....think about it. This baggage also includes your past, guilt, expectations, other people's mistakes, negativity, hurt, trauma, and or disappointment. Cheers to making the choice to LIVE!

This book is being written to address the fact that we all may have been dealt a not so favorable hand in life, but the reality and truth is, we all have two choices to make, either do something about it or don't. It really is that simple. It gets to a point in your life where you are either going to cry about your situation or you're going to change your situation. Courtney here, If you haven't noticed by now I am very straightforward, there is no way to sugar coat the truth, there is no pad to soften the blow, it is what it is. Jenn mentioned how we first met, I really did send her a DM. I was looking to connect, not only with a like minded person, but someone I could collaborate with, and make things happen. The reality is that two people are better than one when it comes to bringing people together, and bringing an idea to life, so I took a chance and reached out, and here we are! If you want something, go get it, that has been my life's motto. No mountain too high or valley too low. Please join us as we share our journey, experiences, and perspectives on life. We are opening up to reveal pieces of ourselves that have been hidden, and protected for so long, in the hopes of inspiring our readers to take the next step, get back up, never give up, and go after whatever it is they want.

FOOD FOR THOUGHT: Things are going to happen in life. How you respond to these things is your choice

CHAPTER 2

Doing your work

Lauren Hill aka L. Boogie said: How ya gonna win, if you aint right within?! This means no matter how good you may look on the outside if your internal emotional state isn't right, it serves you no good. Doing your work, helps create a better version of you. It also aids in living a more fulfilling life. Simply put: one of the greatest things you can do is invest in yourself. This looks different for everyone. For some, it may be going to school. For some, it may be reading. For some, it may be working through past issues. For some, it may be journaling. For some, it may be meeting with a mentor. For some, it may be a combination of all of the above; and possibly much more. There are no shortcuts to doing your work. Life happens to all of us, including me. Something I tell my clients is that I also have to continue to do my work. In addition, I encourage them to trust the timing of their journey and their process. Don't compare yourself to others or what they seem to have or don't have. Simply put, everything that glitters isn't gold. Additionally, living in a grateful state has worked well for me. When you are content with what you have the universe rewards you with more of what you want. Law of attraction. The goal is getting to a place of peace and truly understanding that what's meant for you won't pass you by.

With that being said, there is something magical about finding out who you REALLY are. The real you outside of your family, relationships, social status, degrees etc. Life's adversities happen in order to mold us into who we are truly destined to be. However, so many people can't identify what their likes/dislikes are, what excites them and/or what sets their soul on fire, and to ask/seek help when they need it. So many people are numb from life's happenings. There is no shame in seeking help and growing. Growth can be a beautiful thing. Reflecting, as I often do, I'm so grateful for where I am today. How did I get to where I am today? I did my work and am committed to being a lifelong learner. I am open to what the universe has for me and sends to me. It's daily, actually. If you just quiet the noises of drama, toxic people, unrealistic expectations of life, listen and pay attention. That doesn't mean I don't have my moments. I am human and so are you. What I do know for sure is that you do not have to be a product of your past or your environment. You can break generational trauma and curses. You can change. It is never too late. Nothing good, bad, or indifferent lasts forever. People make choices. I am people. You are people. We are people. The choice is yours.

Mommy/Daddy issues: I was conditioned at a young age to think these terms applied to people that didn't have both their parents around. I want to publicly apologize for that way of thinking and respectfully argue that we ALL have Mommy/Daddy issues. In fact, those of us that did have both of our parents around are overlooked for that very reason. We all have a story. We all have a journey. We all have things we think our parents should have or shouldn't have done. We are all human. The healing comes in when you confront these feelings and process them. In doing my own work, I have resolved to know, process, and accept that my parents did what they could with the tools that they had. Just because they are my parents, doesn't mean they aren't human first and are perfect. I want to encourage you to look at things today through a lens of compassion and inspire some food for thought. How did your parents show up? What was their story? Did they heal their past issues? Was it passed to you? Only person you can control is yourself. You can help make your future better by doing YOUR work. The flip side of this--your inner child, will continue to show up screaming for attention. This sometimes appears as a meltdown, depression, anxiety, and unhealthy toxic behavior in relationships, etc. I promise you this--there is so much peace and joy on the other side of healing. Break the cycle. Start making changes and start living your best life, today. Even a small change can start you in the direction you need to go. When you have set-backs or bad days, take the time you need to get yourself together but don't stay there too long. Don't forget that you are human. It's okay to have a melt down. Just don't unpack and live there. Cry it out and then refocus on where you are headed. Remember we have a life to LIVE.

People tend to hide behind their scars, but I've found that releasing 'your truth' is freeing. I know some people think this is scary but *fear* is an illusion. Let me explain. Think about a time when you were so terrified to do something. You may have had butterflies, anxiety, etc. Once it was over that sense of relief comes over you and more often than not you can admit that you were worried for no reason. Although, I say fear is an allusion, I know it can sometimes paralyze us from growing or embracing change because we get comfortable in what's uncomfortable. Fear can have two meanings. Forget everything and run or face everything and rise. The choice is yours. Find what you are afraid of, face it, and then you won't be afraid of it anymore. One of my favorite mantras is "Worry is interest paid on a debt you may not owe." Moreover, it does take courage to live in your truth, but I believe in you. In talking about these matters you may find that you have things in common with someone else this may lead to a process of overcoming and a healing experience. If you're not ready to release your truths publicly start with someone such as a therapist, life coach, mentor, trusted friend, or in your journal.

For me, doing my work included and includes so many tools. I have a therapist and have had various ones over the years. I want to point out that several people have said to me, "I tried therapy and it wasn't for me. I didn't like my therapist." I counter offer this food for thought, often times we go through several hair stylists, nail technicians, and mechanics before we find one that we like, works for us, or meets all of our needs. Use this same school of thought when it applies to your mental health and finding a therapist that works for you. I also have life coaches, several mentors, and spiritual advisors. I journal, I travel, I work out, I date myself, I do research, I practice self care, I read, I journal, I observe, I self reflect, I check myself, and I apologize. Doing your work is not a destination but rather a journey. It's trial and error. Seeing what works and what doesn't. Let's make a conscious choice to do our work and vibrate higher and higher. To this day, hearing family stories is so magical to me. I would ask, and still ask a lot of questions about both sides of the family. This served as a dual purpose for me. I loved hearing about my legacy, but these stories helped me fill in the blanks and put various puzzle pieces together. Why did certain things happen? Why were my parents the way they were? Were there reasons why my parents had the financial issues they had? Through my research I have gotten answers to some of my questions and others I have made peace with the Type A personality in me that always seeks closure and wants things to make sense. I realized that some things don't matter. I hope my self-disclosure throughout this book blesses, inspires, and encourages someone. Again, this is serving a purpose of shedding light on how and why I show up the way I do in this lifetime.

Healing the inner child. What does this mean? When I started therapy years ago, I thought I was going to deal with the loss of my Dad. I later found out that this went far beyond just losing a parent. I had to pinpoint where and when I was first traumatized. When was I first disappointed? The first therapist told me that I was running on E and if someone or something didn't fill my tank up I would break down. That was really eye opening for me. I was on cruise control for so long, I guess I didn't realize how bad a shape I was in emotionally and otherwise. I had to go back and dig deep on why certain behaviors were showing up in my adult life and how it was affecting all of my relationships. For example, my relationship with finances. I had to unlearn certain behaviors and recreate ones that served the person present day. I had to go back and love on that little girl and tell her it was okay. Let her process her hurt, broken promises and various feelings instead of suppressing them. It was hard to revisit some of these occurrences. What I will say, once you do, it is so liberating! It is not always easy or pretty but it is worth it.There is so much peace and freedom on the other side of healing and doing your work. I encourage you today to take the first step. Do your own personal work so you can live your best life without the baggage and weight of your past. Repeating the same bad habit over and over again is a form of insanity. There comes a point in your life when you know better, and you have to do better. You owe it to yourself to do better. It is just that simple.

I want to add that healing doesn't have to look magical or pretty. Actually, real healing is hard, exhausting, and draining. Please make space and allow yourself to go through it. Don't try to paint it as anything other than what it is. Be there for yourself without any judgment. You can not hide from your inner turmoil and trauma. You can't surgically remove it. You can't eat, buy, wish it, or exercise it away. You have to turn towards it, embrace it, look it into its eyes. Be patient and tender and then get intimate with it until it shows you another way, a different you. Again, the choice is yours.

<ins>"When there is no enemy within, then the enemy on the outside can do you no harm" -African Proverb</ins>

Doing your work, what exactly does that mean? You may see this and feel your work is done, you may think it means having earned a degree, landing a job, or moving out of "the hood'. However, doing your work has nothing to do with those things, in fact it really isn't anything tangible, it's more like addressing the issues that are holding you back, the problems that keep recurring in your life. For me personally, it was my anger. Growing up my family would have described me as the problem child. I had a short temper, my tongue if possible could cause injury, and if you challenged me, fighting was never out of the question. 1 Corinthians 13:11 When I was a child I talked like a child, I thought like a child, I reasoned like a child. When I became a man, I put the ways of child behind me. For a very long time in my adulthood this was not true for me and in some situations still not, as I am still doing my work. I mean it was a point in my life where I had a career, two degrees, a family, a business and I thought I really had my shit together. I felt as though "Who could knock me down?" The answer was me. You will learn in life, that if you don't do your work, you will end up sabotaging the things you worked for, the relationships you have built, and goals you have reached only to end up back at the starting point or with egg on your face. For me though, I kept finding myself in similar situations where I ended up enraged at the audacity of some random ass person. I mean it was not one time but a total of four times where I was approached on some outlandish issues. From an old woman following me and my son out of the library, only to tell me a sign said no idling. This event may seem small, but the fact she followed me in a parking lot full of cars to my car even though my car wasn't on long enough to enter the address to our destination really messed my head up. On top of that, after explaining I just turned my car on and asking her why she felt the need to tell me about the idling sign, she yells, "Because I care about your child more than you!" The situation really had me worked up and even after processing it, I still thought, "The nerve of her, she cares about my son more than me!" The event played on a constant loop in my head. Then to have that microaggression followed by three more random, out of nowhere situations, when I am minding my own business I took my ass to therapy. For one, because I needed to know what exactly was I doing wrong, how come these situations kept happening to me? Furthermore, why do they bother me for days on end? I was told that I wasn't crazy and that there has been an influx of people coming to therapy because of microaggressions happening to them. Essentially, since Trump became president a certain group of people find it incredibly hard to mind their business. I also learned that I had some trauma from childhood and the psychological response that I developed when I feel threatened is to fight instead of flight. For whatever reason, that made me feel better, but also made me want to work on my anger and address the things that I had no clue were the root of my anger. I decided consciously I didn't want to have an automatic reaction when I could instead respond to situations that didn't threaten my life.

Through a few sessions I was able to analyze and understand myself. I realized that everything doesn't need that much energy, a response, or even acknowledgement. I realized that I didn't have to do everything with so much passion. Tam teaches that "when ever affliction of anger arises we should visualize the principles of compassion, forgiveness and emptiness of all dharmas, and a person with heavy karma who can not suppress their afflictions by the visualization principles alone should use "Phenomena", (an external form), such as leaving the scene and slowly sip a glass of cold water" (Tam 1993). Since learning that I will say it has worked a great deal, it has become a go to coping skill which allows me time to respond and not react. I will not lie, even in practicing this, leaving or removing myself I still felt the stress in my body, tension, and a need for a release. With that recognition, I started to practice yoga, meditation, and mindfulness. I find that it helps to keep me grounded and even keeled, and helps with my anxiety, stress and my anger. Now, I try to hold on to the moments when I am at my calmest and when I am at peace, and when I am happy, so that I can revisit that space and time, when I feel angry, or frustrated.

My advice to anyone who finds that similar situations are recurring, be it failed relationships that are romantic, platonic, or even with family, look at yourself and see where you can grow and what you can do on your part to work on it. Start with yourself. If you feel as though you are constantly the person getting used or walked on, look at why, the cause and the root of where it stems. Anything that is not growing is dead. I am always open to learn, grow, and evolve. Doing your work is not something you will ever finish, it is a lifelong process, with the ultimate hope of being so in tune with who you are, where you're going, and by constantly gaining an understanding of where you have been and what you have been through. We owe it to ourselves, our children, and their children to do our work.

REFLECTION

Some ways in which you can start to do you work is by identifying the root of problems. Ex: If you struggle with low self-esteem, or embarrassment, you might think back to a time you felt ashamed of yourself. What or who made you feel this way? Why? Trace the problems back to where they started. List some areas you feel you need to work on to advance to your higher self.

_____

_____

_____

_____

_____

_____

_____

_____

_____

*FOOD FOR THOUGHT: We attract what we are ready for. Have you healed your inner child? Have you done your work? Your wound(s) are probably not your fault, but your healing is your responsibility *

CHAPTER 3

Resilience

⁘

The late, great Nelson Mandela said you never lose. You either win or learn. I love this perspective. If we use this thought process with the things in life, it takes the pressure off of so many things. Another perspective that a dear soul sister shared with me is to love the heck out of everything. Love where you are, what you are doing, and who you are with. Look around you and appreciate what and who you have. Nothing will be the same in a year. Time waits for no one. We have to choose to live while we are here. Don't wait for a special occasion or time. The time is now. The choice is yours.

I am a product of a two-parent household where my parents were married until my Dad passed away in 2008. For reference points, both of my parents were college graduates, worldly, and grew up in middle-class religious families. They raised my sister and I with morals, such as treating people with respect and being considerate. In doing my work, I do want to note that I was once conditioned to think people's degrees had a lot to do with who they were. I have even made some people inadvertently feel "less than" for this belief I once held. For that, I publicly apologize. I now subscribe to the belief that people should do what is best for them. School is not for everyone. Degrees do not necessarily equal success and for those that work hard for the degree(s) they acquire, they should be proud of the hard work that was put into obtaining them.

My Dad hailed from the Midwest--Kansas City, Missouri to be exact. My paternal grandparents were from the South, Alabama & South Carolina. They were well to do in that day and age, married and had 3 children, two girls and a boy. My dad was the middle child, played sports, and was a graduate of Morehouse college. I understand he was a great son and brother, but quite the jokester & would hit my Aunts with wet dish towels from time to time. After finishing college, Dad also served the United States Armed Forces in the Army branch, before spending all his bachelor years twenty plus in New York City where he met my Mom. My Dad lost my grandfather to Leukemia when he was sixteen and from my understanding stepped into *the man of the house role* afterwards. My Paternal Grandmother, my last living grandparent, passed away when I was just one years old. I have always wondered what it would have been like with living grandparents but loved, and still love hearing stories about them.

By trade, Dad was a sales and marketing business man with an underlying entrepreneurial spirit. Dad had a larger than life personality and made everyone feel comfortable and welcomed. He was a true family man and sports enthusiast through and through. He loved to cook (*he knew his way around the kitchen for sure*), play music, dance, barbeque, and entertain. He taught my sister and I so many valuable life lessons such as being a team player and being considerate. I will give him credit for teaching us to drive and all the lessons surrounding cars (i.e. AAA, oil changes, putting air in a tire, etc). During family road trips, he would get so annoyed when we would fall asleep for too long. This was because he wanted us to see and learn. Another thing that annoyed Daddy was when we wouldn't watch the various parades on TV during Thanksgiving and Christmas holiday mornings. We would rather sleep back then. Present day, I wake up and watch. Dad was tall (*6'4" and handsome--if I may say so myself*), super fun, funny, a great teacher, and great human encyclopedia of just about anything, especially random facts. He knew how to wear a suit and was good at so many random things. My family says I have a lot of his traits, I'll take it.

My dad was not a fan of my sister and I having multiple piercings (*I now have 6*), tattoos (TBD), braids, ashy ankles, popping gum, going out of the house with head scarves on our heads, and the smell of nail polish remover. Before school, our beds should have been made and trash cans should have been emptied. I realized how much of these things stuck with me as I became an adult. It is not that I want to rebel against or *disrespect* everything that I was taught but there is *freedom* in creating your own ideologies. For example, does me getting a tattoo mean I am "bad" person?! How many things that we were taught growing up stem from a belief system that no longer serves us or the times? When thinking about the tattoo question, I've concluded that it was most likely rooted in what people would think if I got a tattoo. I respectfully say, I don't care what people think. People are always going to have opinions. I encourage you to get to a place where your happiness is not rooted in other's opinions. Now if you ask for someone's opinion on something, that is another story. However, if you make the choice to live for others, how will you ever be truly happy? If and when the day comes and I decide to get a tattoo, it will be solely based on my decision.

My Mother is from Liberia, West Africa and did her undergraduate studies at Oxford University in London. My maternal grandparents were married until my grandfather passed away. Mom comes from a family of five siblings, four girls and one boy. Her birthplace being the second to last child. She lost her Father at age seven and her Mother while she was away at Oxford. In Liberian culture, it is not uncommon for extended family to step in during times like this. After these losses, my

Mom was basically adopted by a Paternal Aunt who I hear was super cool and was 'a boss', in terms of owning property and having a bit of coin.

From what I know, My Mom was and is that friend, sister, cousin that everyone went to -- for advice, to have fun, if you wanted a meal, etc. She was an English teacher by trade but after marrying my Dad and coming to the US, she was a stay at home Mom until my sister and I were in middle school. When Mom went back to work, she worked for the board of education for years before going back to school for a computer certification. After which, she worked as an EA in Corporate America until her retirement. She was always a fashionista, according to my Aunts, -- I suppose that's where I get that part of my personality and my looks from. She is an intelligent, religious, caring, devoted, green eyed beauty with supreme wit. She loves to talk on the phone, watch the news, watch soap operas, read, and have debates. She is very passionate about current events, especially politics.

I can still hear a lot of the sayings my Mom would say to us a child--"the habits you form now, will stay with you all your life," "everything that glitters isn't gold," "No one owes you anything," "when someone does you a favor, be grateful and be ready--don't have them waiting for you." I remember the first time I broke up with a boyfriend. She made me apologize, not even knowing the full story. She exclaimed, "Jen, you can't do that. That is someone's son." In transparency, I still stand by my sixteen-year-old decision but will admit I have had a mature conversation with that ex in recent years. I not only think he was one of my journey teachers but happy to report we both apologized to each other for immature shenanigans that transpired in that relationship. Growth is an amazing thing and I am always grateful when life presents opportunities to right my wrongs and grow. It's so freeing!

As a young girl, I remember watching my Mom get ready for work and church. I would watch how she would put certain outfits, shoes, purses together. I would watch how she would do her hair and makeup. This is a huge reason why I dress for work a certain way versus when I go out. Something that I have learned about myself is that as much as I like to dress up, I like being in comfortable clothes. It takes me back to my riding bike-tomboy days. The good ole days--where my biggest responsibility was making sure my homework was done so I could go out to play, but not before changing out of my school clothes into my play clothes. These were the days where our block had all the neighborhood kids outside playing until the street lights came on. Do kids even still play outside? These were my happy times. In addition to riding bikes, we played dodgeball, hide-n-seek, went to the park, made trips to a nearby swamp to collect tadpoles and frogs, jumped rope, played cards, played some video games, created home videos, and had snacks before dinner. We were some creative kids. We once made a hammock out of rolled up newspaper and rope. Then there was our mushroom stew. I can't remember any of the ingredients besides mushrooms from outside, dirt, and mud. I remember a time it stormed really bad and a huge tree fell in my nextdoor neighbors backyard. All of us kids went around collecting pine cones, sticks and other storm debris. We turned that fallen tree into a pretend ship and had a market where "pirates" could "buy" things such as the sticks. I miss those Tower Lane days but whenever I think about those times, I smile.

One of my favorite stories of all time is my parents love story because I am a hopeless romantic, love serendipitous happenings, and of course it's my legacy. I mentioned earlier that my parents met in New York. My Mom was in the U.S. to see a foot doctor resulting from an ongoing, annoying childhood foot injury. She happened to stay with her sister-in-law who was dating one of my Dad's best friends, Uncle Jay-Cee--May he continue to R.I.P. When Uncle Jay-Cee saw my Mom he called my Dad up and said, "Johnny I think you should cancel your plans tonight. You're going to want to meet Liz's sister-n-law." Dad took Uncle Jay-Cee's advice and invited the three of them over to his apartment. Mom says that when my Dad saw her, he extended his hand to her and said, "I am going to marry you." My Mom said she thought he was nuts but I think it was magical that Dad knew what he wanted to marry her and kept his word. They got engaged shortly after this meeting and got married two years later. My parents tied the knot in Liberia, West Africa in March of 1981. During that time there was serious turmoil in Liberia and my parents didn't have much contact being in two different countries and the phones being down etc. My Dad flew over by himself. His friends and family couldn't go for various reasons. They later had a reception in the states for friends and family in the U.S. My Dad was still was going off the wedding date they had previously set the last time he talked to my Mom. I am amazed at this act because I am an advocate for keeping your word. It means so much to me. I'm so grateful for the amazing example of love, marriage and teamwork they taught my sister and I. Two imperfect people, perfect for each other. Two people that chose to keep choosing each other. Wow, when I think about it, it gives me chills! I still believe in marriage and true love because of them. In my professional opinion, one of the best things my Father ever did was to *love* my Mother. As a child, you code things an interesting manner. I can say without a doubt there was a lot of love in my family unit. I could always feel the love. My Dad loved 'his girls' and would show us in various ways. My Dad would tell us how pretty we looked especially on Sundays when we would get dressed up for church since we grew up Christian-Baptist. Love and affection was absolutely present and he adored my Mom. I remember them giving each other back massages in the kitchen, tending to each other's feet, joking with each other. My parents were best friends and taught my sister and I the true meaning of unconditional love. I remember when someone was under the weather, the other would pick up the slack. They shared in household chores and stressed the theme of *"team work makes the dream work."* Societal gender roles were not majorly stressed in my household versus helping each other out. I am in no rush to have children but do look forward to having my own team comprised of my husband and my future children.

My parents were big on helping others out. I remember when certain family members and friends lived with us. I remember taking trips and going to amusement parks. I remember family parties and barbeques. I remember times when the phone, lights, and water were off. I remember waking up on various Christmas mornings when there was nothing under the tree except the skirt. I remember going back to school with the same clothes and shoes from the previous school year. I remember when both parents had health issues. I remember going through financial issues which led us to moving several times including being homeless. I want to clarify my use of being homeless here. Most people would think I mean living on the streets. Although we were not on the streets, we were without a home and therefore I use the word *homeless* here. Our living situations included living with relatives and friends but *mostly* living in motels and hotels. I think this is when I truly understood the concept of it takes a village to raise a child. I am forever grateful for everyone that has and still plays apart of my village.

It was the mid 2000s and I was homeless, living with three other people (my parents & sister) in a local, one bedroom, bed bug infested hotel. I was a full-time college student, working full time and trying to figure out life. I was resentful, lost, and sometimes felt like throwing in the towel. I had no clue what I wanted to do with my life but knew I wanted more for myself. I was beyond frustrated and was tired of moving around. I wanted stability. I was tired of pretending everything was okay when it wasn't. I was numb and looking for an escape.This escape was often hanging out with friends and spending time and my energy with people that didn't deserve it. Little did I know; life was about to get REAL.

During *one* of our *homeless* hotels stays, my family got placed in a room that was infested with bed bugs unbeknownst to us. If you know anything about these creatures; they are not easily visible by sight, they attack at night when you're asleep, and it takes moving heaven and earth to get rid of them. Weeks later, room changing, sprays, powders, washing and throwing away items--the bugs were gone but the scars remained both physical and otherwise. Years later, the scars have faded but I am reminded that when the "bugs" of life appear to bite you, add annoyances to your life, shake up your world, make you question your purpose -- they are temporary even when it seems like there's no solution or way out. These "bugs" come to make you stronger. They come to build your character. When you lay your head down at night, try reflecting on how far you've come, the things you've overcome, and the things you have yet to accomplish. I encourage you to rid yourself of the "bugs" of life and keep it moving. You still have the rest of your journey waiting for you.

There's no question that I'm blessed, but you know what, there's no testimony without a test. I'm here to tell you; there's life after losing a parent. There's life after failing a test. There's life after being jobless. There's life after being homeless. There's life after being broke and broken. There's life after failed relationships. There's life after sickness and surgery. Whatever you're going through today, be encouraged. Nothing good or bad lasts forever. In doing my work, my outlooks on so many things have changed. Maybe spending time in the hotel was forcing us to spend time together. Some of my last memories with my Dad were in one of those last hotels we lived in. Thinking back to that time of my life still isn't great, but I can talk about it without crying. I know it was a part of my journey and I made the choice to work through some of the darkest times of my life. I had to talk to my Mom about feelings that were uncomfortable for both of us. I had to work through my resentment that both parents contributed to with only one parent being physically present. I am resolved that I was once shattered, but I am not broken. I am and continue to be resilient. Will you make the choice to be resilient? Life will happen to everyone. How will you choose to handle and respond to life's one promise: *change*? Remember, the choice is yours.

> *"I think that life is difficult. People have challenges. Family members get sick, people get older, you don't always get the job or the promotion that you want. You have conflicts in your life. And really, life is about your resilience and your ability to go through your life and all of the ups and downs with a positive attitude."*

— Jennifer Hyman

Resilience, what does that mean to you? Is it something that you are born with? Is it something that you gain over time? Is everyone resilient? To answer the last question, no everyone is not resilient. Everyone cannot bounce back after being traumatized, or a major life event. I do however believe that your life events, trauma included, adds to your resilience. I personally am thankful for all that I have been through, it has made me exactly who I am. I don't think I am indestructible, but I know if it doesn't kill me, it can only make me stronger. I am originally from South Philadelphia, where I grew up until we moved to South Jersey with my grandmother. Which is literally only 20 minutes across the bridge, but two different worlds. In South Philly I lived on 6th street and what you would consider the inner city. In Jersey, I lived on a very quiet street with a front yard and huge backyard, and the neighbors were a great distance away. Well, I can officially say I survived the move, adjusted, and adapted reasonably well. I mean you can take a girl from South Philly, but we all know South Philly will forever be in the girl. With this move, it made me see my parents, their flaws, and their addictions. My father, Nate, who used to walk us to school every day, take us to the park, play board games, and seemed a little strict, became almost non-existent. He went from being an everyday involved father, to what I considered in my teenage years; my mother's sperm donor. At the time we all lived together, he may not have been a full-blown alcoholic but soon turned into an alcoholic because he couldn't deal with the reality of my mother leaving him. My mother, April, when we all lived together would have lunch prepared after school, bake cookies with us, and do all kinds of crafts. Though she had her own demons, that as a young child I overlooked because it was my norm. On any given night, my sister and I could wake up to a very cloudy living room and a sheet up to the kitchen. I never thought anything of it, but later realized that the smell that was so familiar to me, was her actually smoking crack. On any random day our jewelry, tv, or radio, would go missing along with our mother. But it wasn't until we moved to jersey and my mother's drugs were not right around the corner that my parents and their addictions impacted me the most. Once my mother left us at a family cookout, we ended up living with her sister for about a year before we heard from her again, and just like that it was a norm. It was the norm, to only hear from April every few months, mostly when she was arrested and needed an address to be released to, she would come to stay for a few months, and then be off again me and my sister referred to them as "missions". There were no warning signs, but eventually you learn to expect it and accept it. The only thing that seemed to bother me was that now it wasn't only my older sister and I. Now we had two younger brothers and I didn't want to see them hurt by it, or her, and her coming and going. My parents still to this day struggle with their addictions. I love them dearly and I wouldn't change either of them for the world. My dad is the most easy going, light hearted guy, he just wants to see people smile. My mother is literally everyone's favorite. She is down to earth, a great cook, has a good heart, and will not hesitate to tell you like it is, she in the sense of every word is a hustler, she will make a way always, I get a lot of my characteristics from her. What my experience has taught me is that people at their core are not their mistakes, shortcomings, or their choices. My mother didn't leave us because she didn't care, she left because she knew that we wouldn't be safe where she was going. My father never stopped loving us but his own pain and lack of resilience kept him from being that everyday father. Because of both of them I can honestly say that parenting for me is something that I take very personally. I love being a mother, to me there is no greater gift. Because of my childhood I could have easily used it as an excuse not to try, to give up, and accept whatever life gave me. Resilience is the opposite of trauma and the ability to adapt well to adversity, tragedy, threats, or even significant sources of stress. When I think about life and what I have learned so far it is that resilience is something that can be strengthened through living and learning from mistakes. Other than the events of my childhood, which I think has helped build my resilience, the challenges in my adult life have also added to it. When I speak on my experiences in life people's response is "oh you have lived a life", and it's true I have…. When I think about my experiences in my adulthood my mind goes to my two divorces as well as two bankruptcies. Now, before you go judging, please just hear me out. I married young at 23. If I am being honest, I was caught up with the idea of how things should be, and I thought that there was a clear map to what I wanted and where I was going. I thought life was black and white, I should be married and travel, and then I should start a family. I thought love was enough to make it through anything. What I didn't know was that marriage is 1.) A financial merger, truly we didn't have the same understanding of being responsible with bills, and money. Even before I married him I filed bankruptcy because when I went away to college I lost control of my credit card accounts, no one told me to stay away from credit card debt, I was working 3 jobs but couldn't afford to pay the minimum to maintain them. That was a major lesson for me, but for my first husband, if you had it spend it all, with no thought of the future to save. 2.) People are constantly changing, evolving, and growing, or not. I was the one that was changing, evolving, and growing, while my first husband was not, well not at that moment. My growth scared him, and him being complacent and content scared me. With this marriage I learned how strong I was, I managed and maintained my lifestyle just the same as when we were together, I continued to progress, and succeed.

With my second marriage, came many things, a lot of highs and a few lows. This time in my life I thought this man was heaven sent. We had the same work ethic, we planned and built together. We had our first home built from the ground up and I started three businesses with him by my side. He was very supportive in that aspect. We had a plan for him to open his own auto body shop but before that could happen, he ran into some legal trouble. The thing with this plan, was that we didn't have a backup plan and the legality of the situation kept us from moving forward. For him it was a downhill spiral that he couldn't seem to recover from, and

I wasn't in the position emotionally to provide what he needed without hurting myself. From that marriage, I had my first child and the biggest blessing to my life. I had to leave behind my house, my husband, and my lifestyle only to start over once again. The ability to start over again is where the resilience comes in. I mean I have met people who never recover from a break up, let alone a divorce. A divorce is where what was supposed to be a forever thing, gets flipped upside down. You are left with no choice but to regroup and start over, all while trying to ensure consistency for your child in hopes of not traumatizing him. Having a plan is important and it helped a lot. In my situation I needed to relieve myself of the things that tied me and my soon to be ex-husband together, house included. I had to free up my money so that I can start putting it towards the future. I filed bankruptcy for the 2nd time, it hurt just a little because at the time my credit score was in the 700's, but not that much because I knew it wouldn't take long to rebuild. I then moved into a spacious one bedroom, something that I could afford on my own and that would leave me room to save and regroup. One year, after saving I was able to move into a two bedroom townhome, now today almost two years later I have rebuilt my credit to a 700. I am going to purchase my first property by myself with the plan of making it the first of many investment properties. In retrospect, what did I lose? Nothing! I put my happiness first, I survived and I am exactly where I am supposed to be. I am the product of an alcoholic and a crackhead, if we were to minimize my parents down to their addictions and poor choices. Yet, I am more than that I am the product of my struggle, and my motivation to live this life in full. "I am not the sum of my circumstances, but the product of my choices." -Stephen R. Covey

REFLECTION

Are You Resilient? There are 5 characteristics in regards to resilience. They are adaptability, self-control, self-sufficiency, optimism, and persistence. In short adaptability is the ability to accept change and continue to function at a high level of performance. Self-control is the likelihood of an individual's judgement or behavior being affected by emotions or desires, ability to make rational decisions, even when faced with complications or difficulties. Self-sufficiency is considered to include the ability to work autonomously without the need of guidance or relying on others. Optimism is the outlook in regards to the negative or positive view. Finally, there is persistence which looks at the ability to overcome difficulties and can indicate a willingness to work hard and offer additional efforts when required.

How do you deal with setbacks?

_____

_____

_____

_____

_____

How do you cope under pressure? Recognizing how you cope will allow you to adjust. Some people eat, others shut down, some have anxiety attacks. As for me, I make a plan.

_____

_____

_____

_____

_____

What has been your biggest "failure" to date and how did you deal with it?

_____

_____

_____

_____

_____

FOOD FOR THOUGHT: Life's a journey, not a race. This journey will have setbacks but also comebacks. When life changes to be harder, change yourself to be stronger

CHAPTER 4

Happiness is a journey; finding your happiness

❧⸻❧

You're going to be happy said life but first I'll make you strong. Most people will choose a familiar misery over a forigen happiness. In general, people want happiness but either don't know what it looks or feels like or they are too scared to get to that place because of various reasons. These reasons include but are not limited to fear and being too comfortable in your unhappiness. I encourage you today to make a step towards finding your happiness. Get out of that relationship that no longer serves you. Take a chance on the love you deserve. Leave, but be responsible about it, with that job or position you're miserable in. Break that cycle that is yielding the same non-beneficial dividends. Move, travel, take time for yourself-- whatever being happy looks like to you, I want it for you. Listen, life really is too short to be anything but happy. I'm so grateful that I learned this at a young age but remember it is never too late to make a change. You have that choice. According to Life and Mind coach, Vex King, avoiding what you are naturally attracted to, so that you can live in accordance to other people's expectations, will only lead to a life of regret. One secret that I have learned about happiness, is letting every situation be what it is, instead of what you think it should be. Eventually you will get to a place where you are at peace with your past, where you're in love with the person you're becoming, and where you trust God's plans so much that you know whatever is ahead, is far better than what was left behind.

I can't pinpoint the day or time but one day I woke up differently. I was doing my work. I was on the pursuit to find my happiness and I realized that would not come from material things or from someone else. It would not come from escaping or hiding from the ugly stuff. In addition to working through the past trauma, hurts, and disappointments, I started dating myself. I had to find my own happy. This was two-fold for me; I was preparing for future relationships and I wanted to be ready for what life was going to give me. I believe that when you pray for something you should be ready to receive it. If you are not in a ready position, then you should be getting ready. So, I started spending time with myself and by myself as a part of my self-care. I literally took myself out to eat, shopping, to the spa, to the salon. Maybe for you it will be to treat yourself to ice cream or another treat, etc. I would like to note that dating yourself does not always mean spending money. There are alternatives -- you can go to the library, take a walk, sit by a body of water, read a book, take a bath, light candles, listen to music, and journal to name a few. However, the way I look at this, if you could spend some money on someone else or on other non essential things, why not on yourself? You deserve it. You deserve all the good things life has to offer. Everything in moderation. I also find that dating yourself is part of learning yourself. If you don't know yourself and what you like or don't like, how can you expect the universe to be clear on what to give you...whether that be in a life partner, if that is your desire, or just in general.

A lot of people are carrying people, places, and things that are weighing them down. Releasing this baggage is part of finding your happiness. Holding baggage is expensive. The cost of this can be depression, anxiety, and wasting days of your life that could be spent on happy things versus the heavier stuff. I do think it's important to process the less than favorable things that we experience. There is no time limit on how long these things take, however I think it's so important that you don't stay and live in this place. I personally know that this can be so frustrating. Remember, happier and lighter times are awaiting. I am about to share with you an intimate account of the day my life changed forever. Writing this brought up some raw emotions and I think it always will. If you have ever experienced loss, you can relate. I am using this as an example of how you really have to work and fight through the difficult moments of life. Just like there is sun after rain, there are happier times on the other side of sadness and despair.

October 23, 2008. We were still living in a local hotel. This time the hotel was set up more like a one bedroom apartment. My parents had the bedroom and my sister and I slept on the pull out couch in the living room. I felt my Dad's hand on my feet as he left to drop my Mom off to work. It wasn't a tickle but kind of a love tap. He was a gentle giant when it came to us. I mentioned earlier that my Dad had very unique ways of showing his love for us. This was just another one. Some of his sayings and doings were definitely *strange* but I am woman enough to admit I miss him and them terribly. Kellye and I have carried on some of these strange behaviors. I'm sure our friends can vouch for this especially with the various sayings and nicknames we come up with. Dad's one nickname for me was Jenny Lukes, Jenny Lucas, or Jenny. I have no idea where he got the Lucas and Lukes part from, but for years after his passing I wasn't a fan of people calling me Jenny. I am happy to report, I am over that, for the most part, now. Anyway, back to that day -- I was pseudo sleep and although I was cognizant enough to feel his touch, I didn't actually get up because my alarm would be going off soon and I would need to get ready for an 8:00am class. That foot touch was My Dad's way of not waking us up entirely but saying see you later and I love you. I just knew that later on I would get that "annoying call" asking us what we wanted for dinner or something similar where he would call us usually while we were in class. I want to note that he was still learning how to text at this time so his way of reaching out to my sister and I, was to call our cell phones. That was the last time My Dad would physically touch me. That morning, that last foot touch was his way of saying *Goodbye*. As I am writing this, I am realizing where my despise for goodbyes stemmed from. It's so final. That day my world seemed to stop. It felt like I was in a haze and have just been living but the roof off *my house* is no longer there. My superman, my protector, my Dad would be physically gone. It's a void that will never be filled.

Instead of waking up to my alarm, I woke up suddenly from my cell phone ringing. I answered and the person on the other end was my Maternal Aunt. I heard her say "Your Dad had a heart attack!" I think I went into a *safe mode* (like a computer-- running but all the functions aren't accessible) then. There are things I remember and others I don't. I was later told that my response to my Aunt giving me the news was to yell back explicatives. I apologized to my Aunt but will say I don't consciously remember my response. Something else I later found out was my Uncle, my Aunt's husband, was the last number my Dad dialed on his cell, they were very close, and hence why the cops called my Uncle first. I do remember waking my sister up. I told her to wash her face, brush her teeth, and throw something on. In the meantime, I called my Dad's phone. Someone answered right away and hung up. I felt a sense of relief. These people must have made a mistake. My Dad just picked up and must have dropped the phone when I called him. I called back. This time a man's voice that I was not familiar with answered. I said, "Hello, I am John Gregg's daughter." His response to me was, "I would get to Jefferson Hospital now." He didn't give me much more information. I tried asking more information. He hung up. I called back. No answer.

I told my sister to call my Mom, as I brushed my teeth, washed my face and threw on some sweats. Mommy sounded so calm and had no idea what was going on. I got another sense of relief. This can not be as serious as it sounds. I then called my Mom's co-worker and asked her to go to Jefferson Hospital with my Mom and that my sister and I were on our way and would meet her there. I probably should not have driven that day. I don't remember the drive over the bridge from Jersey to Philly. GPS systems were not as great as they are today and it seemed to take forever to get to the hospital. When we finally got there, we parked, and it seemed like forever to get to the place where we were supposed to be. I do remember as I was parking, I was mentally preparing. I was preparing the speech I was going to give my Dad. I was mentally preparing for how he was going to look. I needed to be strong because they needed me. They meaning, my parents and my sister, and I for one wasn't going to let them down.

While walking up to the entrance of the hospital, we spotted our Mom and yelled out to her. She turned away and started walking in the hospital. We yelled again, "Mom!" This moment was like something out of a movie. We felt as though we just couldn't reach her. When we finally walked in the doors of the hospital, we were greeted by a chaplain, my Mom, her co-worker and others that I can't remember. I had no idea what was going on. I was just ready to see my Dad. The chaplain pulled us in a room. That room was so small and I felt like I could hear everyone's breathing. I felt a thick, heavy energy. I thought they were getting ready to explain what happened and my Dad's care regimen moving forward. Afterall, I had been through this before with my Dad's other surgeries, etc. We get the skinny from the doctor, take him home, nurse him back to health and move on with life, because that's what this Gregg dream team does. I was not prepared for the words my Mom uttered next, "Guys, your Dad is gone." I couldn't breathe and I think I dropped. My sister started crying and after repeating the words over and over again in my head, I immediately went into overdrive. I started making calls. I called my Dad's sisters and his best friends. I called my other family and friends. I called my boss, emailed my professors and my classmates because not only was I going to miss work and class that day but I was in the midst of a group project and I felt bad for not being able to work on my part. I was blessed with amazing people around me that understood my situation. I am forever grateful for all the people that were and have been supportive during this life altering experience. I am also grateful for the guy I was dating at the time, and his lack of support and the other people that have made broken promises to my mom, sister and I. It made us stronger and served as just another life lesson.

Even the people you think won't do you like that, will. People will break promises. People will say some shocking things. People will take advantage of you, we were even asked for money--guess people thought my Dad had crazy life insurance policies, even during times like this. Don't take it personal. It has nothing to do with you but more so everything to do with where they are in life. I found that protecting your energy in times like this is the best way to handle it. Because emotions are running high, it's best to not lash out. I am not saying you can't say anything to these types of people or eventually address it but I would advise waiting until you are in a better headspace. To date, I have not addressed many of the people that I heard talked about my Dad, asked my Mom for money, stood up in the church and made public declarations to be there for us, etc. I chose to let the universe take care of these battles for me, just like these people chose to behave the way they did. My peace is more important but I want to publicly thank these people for showing their true colors. Forgiveness is more so for you than anyone else. These burdens are too heavy to carry. I chose to move on with my life and with the people that want to genuinely be in it.

Before I knew it, the word had spread and family and friends showed up to the hospital. It was nice having the love and support we had during that time. Before we left the hospital that day, we were asked by the hospital staff if we wanted to see our Dad. I wasn't sure at first but decided to. It's an image that will always stick with me. He was in a room in the basement of the hospital. All by himself, he laid there somewhat cold to the touch. He hated being cold. He looked so peaceful. Just like he was taking a nap minus the resuscitation tube in his mouth. I started crying again and struggled with accepting this was my new reality. My first love, my superhero was laying there and that was it. How was this fair? Had we not gone through enough as a family? He wasn't going to make my graduation that upcoming May. He wasn't going to be there to walk me down the aisle. He wasn't going to be the best Pop Pop to my future kids. Before we left the room, my Mom, sister, Aunts and Uncle, joined hands and said a prayer.

When we left the hospital, we went back to the hotel, showered and headed to my maternal Aunt's house. This house served as the meeting place for the next few weeks. That day was also the first time I saw grown men cry. They would take a shot of whiskey, which was my Dad's drink of choice, and then start crying. People came and brought food and spirits, shared their condolences, and shared stories of my Dad. These were stories of his travel, when he was in the army, and just the type of man he was. It really did my heart good to hear these stories. It's so interesting to me. To this day, I still hear various stories about my Dad from my friends and old classmates. It's so warming the legacy and role he played in so many lives. It makes me so proud.

When night came, I was dreading going back to the hotel. My sister and I got in bed with my Mom that night but none of us slept well. I can still hear my mom's cry that night. It broke my heart again. It was a weep and I wanted so bad for her pain to be taken away. For the next ten days of me planning my Dad's funeral, I wasn't sleeping and I lost over ten pounds because I wasn't eating. This was my way of helping. I figured if I could take care of the business part of this ordeal at least my Mom and sister could grieve. We were all doing our best to cope with our new norm. During the day wasn't as bad as night because night time is when all the company left my Aunts house and the three of us were faced with our new void. After the services, after everyone went back to their respective states, and we got settled into our new reality I tried running from my grief. I didn't need to face it...... or so I thought. Out of sight and out of mind is how I was dealing with it. I emptied out my Dad's night stand and wanted to give all his stuff to charity. He was a practical man and we didn't need to keep all of his stuff outside of a few keepsakes. This created tension between myself, my mom, and sister. They processed this differently than I. When we would argue, I would just leave and go hang out with friends or numb the pain another way by drinking, clubbing, etc.

I remember bargaining with myself. Jen, just make it until the end of this semester and you can "deal" with your feelings during Christmas break. I went back to class the first week in November that year. I mentioned this earlier, you cannot run from your baggage. Especially grief. In this case, I did make it until after finals but during this break, I was sleeping 14-16 hours a day. I was losing more weight. Depression set in and I really had no desire to do much of anything. I didn't know what I was feeling but I knew it didn't feel good and I wanted my life to be *normal*, whatever normal meant. I was just so tired, sick and tired of being tired. Tired of the way life had been for so many years, and I wanted to do what I could to ensure my future would be different. I was angry, resentful, miserable, irritable, frustrated and mad at the world.

It's interesting how depression shows up in various people but looking back and putting various things together I would make a professional argument that the depression gene runs in my family; both sides. I would go even further to argue that this gene runs in a lot of families. It just shows up differently in every person. Some signs of depression are very visible and others are hidden. Some people hide their symptoms well. I was one of those people, especially because I was conditioned at a young age to suppress certain feelings and emotions. Some people self soothe with substances. My self soother would be food. I am definitely an emotional eater. The only time this wasn't true was in the loss of my Dad. Other times along my journey when stress has presented itself, I have been known to self soothe with food. According to the National Institute of Mental Health, depression is a common but serious mood disorder. It causes severe symptoms that affect how you feel, think, and handle daily activities, such as sleeping, eating, or working. Symptoms of depression are:

- persistent sad, anxious, or "empty" mood
- feelings of hopelessness or pessimism
- Irritability

- feelings of guilt

- worthlessness or helplessness

- loss of interest or pleasure in hobbies and activities

- decreased energy or fatigue

- moving or talking more slowly

- feeling restless or having trouble sitting still

- difficulty concentrating, remembering, or making decisions

- difficulty sleeping, early-morning awakening, or oversleeping

- appetite and/or weight changes

- thoughts of death or suicide, or suicide attempts

- aches or pains, headaches, cramps, or digestive problems without a clear physical cause and/or that do not ease even with treatment

It should be noted that not everyone who is depressed experiences every symptom. Some people experience only a few symptoms while others may experience many. Depression is one of the most common mental disorders in the U.S. Current research suggests that depression is caused by a combination of genetic, biological, environmental, and psychological factors (Nimh.nih.gov, 2019).

My first therapist suggested I treat my depression with medicine. I told her I would think about it. I went home that day and told my Mom. She begged me not to take the medicine. She called her older sister and they both fasted and prayed for me. I told my Mom I would not get on the medicine but part of the reason I was depressed was that I just had too much on my plate and I needed help. Please know that mental health is just as important as your physical health and in fact the two are related. If you are or have been depressed, I don't think there is any shame in treating your situation with medicine but I do want to point out that there are other methods of treatment. These include but are not limited to:

- Therapy
- being active and exercising
- setting realistic goals for yourself
- spending time with other people
- confiding in a trusted friend or relative
- not isolating yourself
- letting others help you
- expect your mood to improve gradually, not immediately
- postpone important decisions, such as getting married or divorced, or changing jobs, until you feel better

- discuss decisions with others who know you well and have a more objective view of your situation

- continue to educate yourself about depression (Nimh.nih.gov, 2019).

Unresolved trauma and behaviors most likely runs in your family and has been passed down through generations. Often these behaviors present as norms to your family members. They have normalized these behaviors. You do have the choice to heal and pass down new healthy behavior patterns. So many people suffer in silence. For those suffering, please know you are not alone. You're not weird and you should not be embarrassed. Once again, these feelings are not prejudice against age, race, or gender. I encourage you to get the help you need. There is no shame in getting help and healing. You have a choice to break generational cycles. When they say it runs in the family you could tell them, "This is where it runs out." Pain travels through family lines until someone is ready to heal it in themselves. By going through the agony of healing, you no longer pass on the poison chalice to the generations that follow. It is incredibly important and sacred work.

"You will never be happy if you continue to search for what happiness consists of. You will never live if you are looking for the meaning of life."

— Albert Camus

Happiness, there are two people that come to mind when I think about happiness and that is Nate (my father), and Boston (my son), they both wake up happy, I mean with smiles. I consider myself a morning person, but I wouldn't say I wake up "happy" I wake up ready to start the day. I give gratitude and thanks, visualize how my day will go, and then I attack it. My dad and son though they wake up with this zest for life. I admire it, really I do. There was a time I let my father come live with me for about 10 months and he would be up before me in the kitchen cooking and he would say, "Good Morning Courtney Girl!" This greeting and phrase was said every morning. At the time I was helping my father get on his feet and never before this time did I think I had "daddy issues", but there was something that annoyed me about his cheery good mornings. I use to think "I would be happy too if I didn't have to pay a mortgage and didn't have any responsibilities." I was on the phone with my sister and I was really worked up over this. I mean rationally thinking and after I verbalized it, I know I sounded silly as hell, to be mad at my father's happiness, he was happy even though he had nothing. He was happy no matter what. I had to check myself like what about his happiness made me angry? After "doing my work" I found that my source of resentment of his happiness was because I felt I was taking care of my father, someone who in my mind didn't take care of me like he should have. Then me, I am here with all my responsibilities with zero room for error because well I don't have reliable parents to fall back on. I felt like he did not deserve to be happy. After I worked through my feelings and identified the root of my frustration I thought about it. My father is always happy, he is happy when things don't go his way, he is happy even if someone else is upset, he is happy and friendly to everyone he encounters. My father has no worries because he will not allow his spirit to be burdened with worries. My father was happy that he woke up that morning, happy to see his grandson, and spend time with me, my dad is naturally happy, and I appreciate him for it. Boston is literally a ball of happiness, he rarely ever has a bad day and when he does he tells me today I was sad, or mad, and we talk it out. Yet, he doesnt stay with those feelings long and he describes himself as a happy kid, and lights up everyone's day, if only I could bottle it up. What I learned from them is to let it fall off, don't hold on to the shit that doesn't matter, everyday is a new day. I realized that sometimes happiness is how we choose to look at the world.

Prior to this lesson life for me has been a constant effort to get where or what I wanted. I never really slowed down to enjoy the life that I was creating. I was constantly worried about the next part of my life without realizing its the here and now that matters, the things I worked for and wanted were right in front of me.

Yoga and meditation has really helped me on my journey to happiness but it wasn't until I started to practice being mindful that I was able to recognize my happiness as it was unfolding, and what it had been previously. One day (December 4, 2017 to be exact) as I stood on the shore in Zanzibar I had this amazing feeling come over me. I stood in the water with this feeling for a minute and realized it was happiness. This was day 6 of my two-week trip to Tanzania, and I had anxiety about leaving my son, about traveling so far away from home, about contracting the stomach virus, but on this day as I stepped into the water. I had no worries, no care, no anxiety. In that moment I wasn't worried about what could go wrong. I knew my son was in the best hands, and I was able to enjoy being in the moment. At that moment I decided that going forward I was going to live happily. On the plane ride back home 24 plus hours, I cried very long and very hard for the things that I would be letting go when I returned home, I cried for the relationships that I had to end and tangible things I would leave behind, because my happiness was important to me. I realized that there were things and people in my life that did not contribute to my happiness but only contributed to my insecurities, my hurt, and my pain. Happiness is most definitely a journey, but it is also a decision. In life you will discover there is no happiness without pain, you have to sacrifice to be happy. According to Manson (2016), "happiness requires struggle, and grows from problems, as real life long fulfillment and meaning have to be earned through the choosing and managing of our struggles." I am not saying that you must live in pain but ultimately what brings us happiness will also bring us pain.

Becoming a mother, earning my degrees, writing my first book all has given me great happiness. However, childbirth was very painful, those early morning late nights were not easy, and writing a book is mentally and physically draining, but still every single last one of those experiences were worth it. We have to find the things in life that are worth the work, worth the effort, and worth the risk. More likely than not it will be the small things that bring us joy, for me its spending quality time with my children, having autonomy over my work days, residual income from an idea that I just happened to follow through. Happiness will come and go like good days and bad days, "the best we can do is make sure we practice the virtues that give us the best possible chance for happiness" (Buckingham, 2012).

REFLECTION

What are you willing to sacrifice to be happy?

_____

_____

_____

_____

_____

_____

_____

_____

_____

_____

_____

_____

_____

What does happiness look like for you?

_____

_____

_____

_____

_____

_____

_____

_____

_____

What do you enjoy doing? (hobbies, activities, or likes)

_____

_____

_____

_____

_____

_____

_____

FOOD FOR THOUGHT: We repeat what we don't repair. What lesson keeps showing up in your life that you have not learned yet? If you want to fly, give up everything that weighs you down.

CHAPTER 5

The struggle is real but worth it

Difficult roads lead to beautiful destinations, but don't allow your struggle to become your identity. The tough days come to build our character and not every day is glamorous. To get through the toughest days you have to dig deep and push through...run it off, cry, scream, yell. Let the emotions run through you. Take what you need from them and get rid of the rest. I am grateful for each new day as it's a chance for a fresh start. Why do I love butterflies and what they symbolize? Butterflies go through a metamorphosis before they are able to fly. Similarly, we as humans go through a series of transformation presented as trials, tribulations, and tests before we become who we are meant to be. Sometimes this change can be uncomfortable but it's necessary for our growth. Embrace your metamorphosis. God makes no mistakes. I encourage you to start today, you're one choice away from living a better life. I believe in you.

Even with all the work I've done, and continue to do, every time I hear of someone losing a loved one, especially a parent my heart breaks all over again. You really can't understand this type of pain unless you experience it. I'm going on 11 years without my Dad's physical presence and here are some things I'll share with you in hopes it will help someone. I'll rip the band-aid off first and then go from there....

1. This pain/void will never go away.

2. You will be okay.

3. You will adjust to your new reality in time.

4. Do your work.

5. People will say things that may upset you.

6. Grieve and don't let anyone rush your process.

7. This is a journey. Good days and bad.

8. You will get support from people you don't expect versus from those that you do. Don't take it personally. Sometimes people don't know how to act in these situations.

9. It's okay to cry and miss them especially on holidays and special occasions.

10. They would want you to live your life.

My personal self disclosure: every wedding I go to and see a Dad walking his daughter down the aisle, I cry. It's the little things I miss the most: corny jokes, his advice, and his cooking. When I see people with their Dad I get sad because my new reality is I will never have those moments. Please cherish your loved ones while you can. Make peace where you can. Life is too short.

In January of 2014, I broke my first bone. Broken bones are common, right? Especially for athletes?.. or so I thought. Surgery, several doctors appointments, physical therapy, and a permanent screw later, I now know that this was another incident that changed my life. Besides the occasional discomfort, numbing, sleep matters, weather induced pain, I still make a choice everyday to live with this annoyance. In this experience, I learned a lot including sometimes you need to rest. For over three months post surgery, I was forced to sit with myself because I couldn't do much of anything to allow for the bones to heal in addition to the high level of pain I was in. I learned a lot about myself during that time and I realize that there was a silver lining in this happening after all. August of 2019 my sister and I went jet skiing. We had a blast besides me losing a pair of sunglasses. Shortly after our summer fun day, a tidal wave flipped us off of the jet ski into the MIDDLE of the river. This was not my first time falling off a jet ski but getting back on this time was different. This time was post shoulder incident. The point of my sharing this: Life is going to knock you down. Accidents will happen. Waves are going to come. You CAN get back up. You CAN choose to have a positive attitude during the various happenings that are most definitely going to transpire. Thinking back to the jet ski incident, I wonder if I panicked what would have happened. I am constantly reminded that the only thing I can control in this life, is how I show up and how I react to the happenings that are going to occur. I am grateful for each day and all the learning experiences I am provided.

Sometimes when we are in dark places, we tend to think we are buried when perhaps we have been planted to bloom. It's okay to be confused at times. Life has a way of making sense when we just relax and stop trying to figure everything out. I would respectfully argue that you're not really grown until you lose a parent. This loss could be to death, addiction, abandonment, etc. Losing my Father has been the most challenging thing I've had to deal with on my journey to date. I cried a lot in the last decade and I was reminded that crying doesn't indicate that you are weak. It actually cleanses the soul and spirit. Since birth, crying has been a sign that you are alive. In addition, my viewpoint on my loss, this continues to be my guide on why I live my life the way I do. Simply put, you have one life to live. Forgive. Love. Travel. Move. Cherish. Release. Reflect. Grow. The choice is yours.*" Look at my success. I didn't achieve it overnight. It has been the product of many years of struggle, and every year my times have shown gradual improvement." -Mo Farah*

Ever heard that saying anything worth having is worth the struggle? I wholeheartedly believe this to be true. I think there is an appreciation that comes after the struggle, unlike the things that are handed to us or given easily. There is a respect that is earned while struggling, you learn how much you want something, you sacrifice your time, energy, sweat, and sometimes tears for the things you want and desire. Whenever I am going through a difficult and trying time, I always find a moment to be still so that I can reflect on the lesson, the journey, and what is being gained. I am also solution focused so I like to look for plans that will help assist me to getting through it, a problem is always caused by a symptom of something else. I remember getting my first job at Burger King and in Jersey the bus line does not run the same as in the city every 15 min and bus stops are not located at every corner. Lets just say the struggle was getting to and from work without a car and relying on public transportation. Every walk to and from the bus stop I promised myself I would save enough to get a car, and once I did, I would never be without one. One day it happened, I got my first car it was a 1997 Honda Accord. The windows did not roll up, the heat didn't work, but it drove. I treated my Honda like a brand new baby, it served its purpose, and I sold it for double the price that I paid for it. I have not been without a car since. My struggle was not in vain, I know the car is only a possession, its material, but the accomplishment in itself gave me satisfaction. The ease it brought to my life was worth every effort of walking in the rain and snow, and with that struggle came an appreciation.

Today I hold my masters degree simply because I value education. I promise getting it wasn't an easy task. I wanted it, it was a personal goal. It was not obtained for advancement, or any other reason other than I wanted it for myself. I worked for it while parenting, launching and running my own fashion boutique, and working full time as a social worker. I was determined to get it. I did it. I mean me, the same person who was placed in learning disabled classes up until highschool. I wasn't learning disabled, I just learned differently. In sixth grade I had to record myself reading a history chapter, play it back, just so I could answer the questions. My problem was that I focused so much on reading fluently that I couldn't read and comprehend. I read to flow but not to process and understand. When I was young I always worried about being called on and stuttering through the paragraph that when I practice reading it was just to make sure my flow was on point. While obtaining my education my entire educational experience has been to learn what worked best for me to understand a subject, I could not just be told but I truly had to understand. To this day, nothing has changed. I process things differently, I see things differently and I have just mastered my way of learning. I always say I am not suppose to be here, I was counted out statistically, people put me in a box with what they *thought I would be or become, but here I am, not because anything has been handed to me, but because I decided what I wanted and worked my ass off to get it.I take pride in all that I am, all that I have accomplished, and who I am becoming. Adversity is unavoidable, it is necessary, so keep pushing, when you do decide to look back, you will see how far you have come, and that is where the appreciation will come in. When we are faced with struggles we can choose to learn from it, and as we continue to push through it we reveal just how resilient we are, we discover our greatness; stand in it.*

REFLECTION

Until we allow ourselves to be tested we will never know our strength.

Think about where you are now and some of the things you have overcome. (list them below)

THEN   NOW

Ie.

(2017) filing bankruptcy   (2019) in the process of
purchasing my first rental property

_____   _____

_____   _____

_____   _____

_____   _____

_____   _____

What are you currently struggling with? (ie. relationship, problem, decision)

_____

_____

_____

_____

_____

FOOD FOR THOUGHT: Give yourself credit for the days you thought you couldn't make it and did.

CHAPTER 6

Relation[ships]: where are "we" going? -- your circle & support

"The soul dries up without company of the good" -Gandhi. Know yourself well enough to avoid the people, places, and things that take you back to the habits you worked so hard to break. Don't personalize or internalize other people's behaviors. What they do is not a reflection of you. Their actions represent them and where they're at in their growth. Just observe instead of getting caught up and overreacting. You will be too much, too loud, too soft, too this, too that for some people. This applies to family, too. Do yourself a favor and stop going around people that don't like you or make you feel like you don't matter. Live in peace. You will always be "perfect" for your people or your tribe. Surround yourself with people who push you to do better in a healthy way. No drama or negativity. Just higher goals and higher motivation. Good times and positive energy. No jealousy or hate. Simply bringing out the absolute best in each other.

I recently had a conversation with a dear friend. He told me that he needed new friends and this wasn't the first time he had disclosed this. I asked him what was stopping him? Guilt? Fear of acting *brand new*? I told him that falling back a bit didn't mean that he was acting funny or had ill will towards these certain groups of people. How much more time would he waste spending time with these people out of force or guilt? What do you have in common other than time? I think so many of us get to this crossroad with the various relationships in our lives. It is okay to change and grow up. Sometimes we outgrow people, places, and things. Another good friend recently shared an analogy with me. Would you stuff your foot into a shoe that no longer fit? No, then why do we do that with other things we outgrow? You have to learn what is best for you and sometimes this means *losing* people along the way. The people that are meant to be in your life for a season will drop off and those that are meant for the long haul will stay. You cannot feel guilty about growth. People will always have opinions and feelings about you but that is not your concern and you honestly can't pay bills with those opinions. Another way to think about this is we are all in a play called life. You are the leading star and director. You will have actors that come and go. The plot will change. The characters will change. The story line will change. Change and growth is inevitable. Think about it. The choice is Yours.

I am grateful to have some amazing friends but in transparency it has taken work. Not everyone can receive what you give. Some relationships are worth working on and others are not. That is up to you to ultimately decide. Difficult conversations, showing up, respect, mutual support, are all involved in what I consider to be a good relationship (of any kind). You also have to be able to take criticism, apologize, and be able to self-reflect. Relationships can not be one sided because eventually the person carrying all the weight will get tired. I have been stabbed in the back, lied to, stolen from, betrayed, talked about, called names, publicly humiliated, and it was by people that I would have least expected. I had to process these hurts and realize that these things weren't happening to me but instead happening for me. It was part of my journey and growth. It was strengthening my muscles. I made the choice to move on with life. Are you choosing to give people too much power over your life and feelings? You are the CEO of your life and it's your job to promote, demote and dismiss people accordingly.

Picture this--a bunch of wires--under a computer desk--that are super tangled up. My emotional state could be compared to these wires, when I met him (an ex) years ago. From the outside, I did a great job covering up what was underneath: a mess. I now know, the law of attraction is REAL. Like me, he looked good from the outside but had a lot of unhealed scars, resentment, and internal conflict going on in the inside. As time went on, we became entangled in each other's webs of toxicity. This included broken promises, hurt, lies, betrayal, -- not to each other-- but instead from the remnants of what took place in our lives before meeting one another. Over the years of our relationship, we found solace in each other's hurt and built a friendship and love based off of turmoil. Usually in disorder, there is chaos and it generally must come to a head.

One day, I was over this unhealthy means of a relationship. I wanted more and deep down knew I deserved more. It must be noted that I am grateful for this part of my journey because this individual served as one of my many journey teachers. Without these lessons, I would not be where I am today. Relationships often give you a mirror reflection of yourself. It's good when you can self-reflect and grow from life's lessons. From this piece of self-disclosure, I not only encourage you to do your work but also to be aware of what kind of energy and vibes you give off. It doesn't matter how good your outer package looks, how you dress, what kind of car you drive, etc. You attract what you're giving off inside. Be okay with being single. Learn what you like and dislike. Hopping from one person to the next without working on your "stuff" will only prolong the growth process. How long will you walk around carrying the weight of past "stuff?" Release it. Work on being a better you so when God sends you "your person" you'll be ready. It happens when you least expect it. Lastly, learn when it's time to walk away from something or someone when it isn't good for you. Don't live in fear of the unknown or what will happen if you stay or don't stay in a relationship you've outgrown. Embrace the timing of your life's journey: becoming who you are meant to be. Will Smith said that God placed the best things on the other side of fear. I couldn't agree more.

"The wrong relationships teach you how to recognize the right one when it arrives" -unknown

Relationships require trust, honesty, respect, communication, loyalty, happiness, compromise, safety, independence, and partnership (Neustaeter 2016) . There are 5 forms of relationships, romantic, platonic, self, professional, and family, (Hamon 2019). Relationships are not easy and they all require time and energy. Some are vastly more important than others naturally, and at times we treat even the most important connections as though they aren't all that important. Does any one relationship come to mind that could use a bit more attention now? If so, be mindful to invest yourself in it to a deeper degree.

I have friendships that I have had for over 20 years, friendships that were built in college, some in my professional life, and others on my entrepreneurial journey. Some of those friendships have turned into family-ships. I have a set of friends that are considered my cousins because that's how intertwined our family is now, our children are now cousins. I have friends who I can be around when I simply want to be by myself, words are not needed, it is understood. I have friends I can call to bounce ideas off of and others I can call and vent to. In some cases I am able to do all of the above with several of those people, and it's just a vibe. I have relationships where I speak to specific people daily, that includes my sisters, my besties, and my cousins (we have a cousin chat). Others several times a week, and others 3-4 times a year, and with all of them we pick up where we left off. I value each relationship that I have had and what they taught me. I love looking at where they started and what they have become. I believe that people come into your life to help you get through, learn, or overcome something. My parents for instance were exactly what I needed to be who I am. Our relationship is not that of a fairytale by any means but it's honest, we have open communication, its safe, and I can trust them to be exactly who they are. I wouldn't change our relationship for the world. As I sit here and type this my mother is in Florida serving her last few weeks in Polk County Jail. We talk via SMARTJAIL mail a few times a week, she's excited about me being with child and coming back to New Jersey to increase her proximity with us. If it is true, that history repeats itself then she will be home for a few months to a year. I can't dwell on that. I have one mother, I accept her as she is, and I trust that she will do exactly what she has always done. I respect that we can talk about anything, and she will always keep it 100. My mother never sugar coated anything and even in her absence she managed to learn all of her children in and out. As well as she managed to teach us all something valuable. Whenever I am going through a difficult time I think to myself "I am April's daughter, I will survive", and then I do. I admire my mother because even as someone who has used drugs on and off throughout my life she has always been true to herself, and has always made a way. I believe there are bonds created in the womb that can not be severed only strengthened. All of my relationships are like that for the most part. We are who we are, we have our connections and I don't push past that if it's not organic. With me there is no judgment for you to be who you are, and I ask for that same respect as I move throughout my journey. That is not to say you can not hold me accountable, you can not correct me if and when I am wrong, or you or I have to put up with toxicity in the name of "this is who I am". Thats where respect for each other, trust, and communication comes in to play.

If you have encountered me in person I can say for certain you have met the real me. You can put me in the room with my grandmother, my boss, and my best friend and you will get the same person. Depending on how high up in the professional world I am, I will adjust, as I am still a professional. Yet still, my point is I am direct, straight to the point, an open book, and I am honest.

Relationships are hard, because they require two people to communicate, understand, interact, compromise, and sync. Even relationships with ourselves are hard as they still require the same. When we are challenging ourselves to grow and evolve that means we are challenging all that we know in our world, adding or subtracting things that no longer serve us, which presents a conflict a struggle between who we are and who we are becoming. According to (Gottman 2002) conflict is normal in relationships, the key is learning the skills to work through that conflict, and one of the best ways is to learn how to communicate. One day long ago I was attending church, and the pastor spoke on a proper way to argue. I remember laughing in my head, at the thought of "yeah go for the jugular", but he went on to say that listening to what each other had to say was the proper way to argue. He explained that if each person is talking at the same time nothing is being heard. If someone is speaking, listen to understand them, and when you respond it should not be with what you think, but to clarify what you think you heard. Then once you have a proper understanding of what was being said, then respond. I thought hmm that will take a lot of energy, but I tried it. I tried it on my grandmother, guess what, it worked. I started to use this technique, and later during one of my courses of study I came across this book by James Petersen named Why Don't We Listen Better? This book is about communicating and connecting in relationships. He spoke deeper on the concept that the pastor spoke on many years prior, and even created cards called TALKER LISTENER that listed the roles of each member. As a talker (Petersen 2007) states should be sharing "I am most bothered by," "I own the problem", the goals of the talker is to share their feelings, and thoughts without accusing, attacking, labelling, or judging. As the listener Petersen states they should be thinking "I am calm enough to hear", " I don't own the problem", and their goals, are to provide safety, to understand and to clarify without agreeing, disagreeing, advising or defending. According to (Steward 2012), there are five steps in preparing to argue. Yes, you read that correctly 5 steps to prepare to argue (Who knew!?) Those steps include:

1. *Asking yourself if the issue you are thinking of is actually a present issue or merely one you have been reminded of.*

2. *If the issue is unquestionably a present one, try to let it go. This must be accomplished thoroughly and honestly or the issue will continue to grow like mold.*

3. *Consider if this is the time (if you feel an urge to bring it up quickly, be very alert to anger) your heart is willing to wait but your ego is not, especially if it senses an opportunity to strike back.*

4. *Be certain that communication is your aim. Trying to get someone to change is not communication because you have already decided what change is needed.*

5. *The final point to consider is whether you are clear that the problem is the relationships and not the other persons. For example: Mary learns that John has made time during his day to start a band, Mary is upset because she feels that the time John decided to commit to the band could have been used for spending time with her or things she wanted to do. Mary needs to assess if this is a Mary problem or if this is a John and Mary problem.*

I shared these two tools with youth as they are great to have and add to your tool box as we are always communicating, and with more practice it will become second nature.

As I said earlier, I value all of my relationships, and I have taken great effort to grow as a person, and with the people in my life. I do not discard of people because we don't agree on everything, or because they challenge me or my beliefs. The only thing that will make me leave a person where they are at, is if their energy does not match mine, if they are constantly draining me, or if it is too toxic for me to maintain and that applies to whomever from family, platonic, romantic, and business. Remember though no man is an island, relationships are important, they serve a purpose, and they all should be going somewhere. Some relationships grow and others are outgrown, appreciate them, the journey, and the lessons for what they are and were.

REFLECTION

What relationships do you value?

_____

_____

_____

_____

_____

What are some of the attributes you admire in each relationship ?

_____

_____

_____

_____

_____

What relationships do you want to improve, and with whom?

_____

_____

_____

_____

_____

_____

Are there any relationships that drain you?

_____

_____

_____

_____

_____

*FOOD FOR THOUGHT: At this very moment, forgive yourself. For the mistakes you've made. For the way you allowed people to treat you before you knew your worth. For not realizing you are great, you are loved, and most importantly you're enough. It was all apart of your journey.

CHAPTER 7

Boundaries & protecting your energy: you are the CEO of your life

I am the CEO of how I respond to things that transpire in life. Guess what? Same goes for you. We give too many people the power to lower our vibrations. Stand true to your own frequency. Remember that sometimes light attracts moths and your warmth attracts parasites so you have to protect your space and energy. Just like you would protect your belongings, or a loved one or another prized possession, guard your energy with all you can. Be selfish on who you share it with. Pay attention to how you feel around certain people. This includes family. Would you keep eating something that made you sick or that you were allergic too knowing the consequences? The same would go here. Pay attention. Your soul knows best. You just have to listen and feel. I know that being around certain people is not always unavoidable but remember everything in moderation and you ultimately have the choice. You are the boss of you. Do what is best for you. Honor and respect your feelings and boundaries.

Believe it or not, I am not a phone person. It actually has become a running joke with my friends and loved ones. Those that know me, know I have to be in the mood to talk on the phone. Otherwise, I prefer to text or email. This is kind of ironic considering I am a life coach and I meet with most of my clients via the phone, right? Well, this was yet another self discovery I've made. I have to make boundaries in order for me to not constantly be running on empty. If you always let people take, they will. It's nothing personal but remember you have to protect your energy. When you're on E these same takers will seldom be around to help fill your tank back up. Use discretion here.

Speaking of self discovery, I do not love reading but I do because I like to learn (yes, I am a total dichotomy in so many areas of life). When I do read, my preferences for books would be in the self-help realm. I have read all types of self-help books and I would say the ones surrounding relationships have been my favorites. It helps me stay current on client issues and the times but also helps me in my own personal relationships. Years ago, I read a relationship book that offered a great way to view relationships. I have used this ideology ever since and it has helped me create boundaries and protect my energy. This perspective states that all relationships (romantic, professional, friendly) are an energy exchange. Each connection either feeds us power or depletes and drains our energy. If we saw all of our relationships from this perspective, we would see that "toxic ties" are those attachments that cause us to lose personal power. The associations we form have the capacity to nurture and inspire our growth, catapulting us into being the best that we can possibly be. However the flip side is also true (Thomas 2007.)

You should balance your energy exchanges just like you would budget your paycheck. Life is about balance. Be kind, but don't let people abuse you. Trust, but don't be deceived. Be content, but never stop improving yourself. Start ignoring people who threaten your joy. Literally, ignore them. Say nothing. Do not invite any parts of them into your space. Be strong enough to let go and wise enough to wait for what you deserve. I have learned that some relationships are worth working on, fighting for, and loving through. Some can bounce back after busy spells, disagreements, hurt, and some are meant just for a teaching lesson. Matters of the heart are never easy but use your discernment. Everything always works out and time reveals all. Ultimately, the choice is yours.

"Energy doesn't communicate in English, French, Chinese or Swahili, but it does speak clearly."

-Elaine Seiler

Have you ever met someone and for whatever reason you steered clear of them because something didn't sit right with you? Most likely that was your intuition telling you that their energy was off. In my past I worked in a group home and before the shift would start, the day shift staff would gather for a meeting. Whenever I enter a room I say a general "Good Morning" out of respect, but I would only engage with those I had a friendship with, while others would be strictly business. One day an older lady asked me, "Courtney how come you don't talk to me?" I paused, and thought well its not cause she older, its not that I don't like her, I don't know her not to like her, then I responded, "I don't know, I didn't feel drawn to you, my spirit didnt take to yours, therefore I left it at that." I told her it was nothing personal and from what I have seen she seems to be a good staff member, I just had no reason to talk to her. Have you ever had an interaction with someone that has left you drained, tired, feeling sad, stressed, or hopeless? I call those people energy zappers. Some may have the intention of doing just that and others may have no clue they are doing it. Along this journey of mine I have learned that energy is real, it is transferable, it is practically everything. I learned that when I give my energy to something, I feed it and when I take my energy away, I starve it. That holds true for everything be it a situation, a person, a relationship, or a project. You see I have some really awesome people in my life, my sisters are slow to anger, I would watch them in amazement, trying to figure out how they maintained their cool. I low key thought, "Oh yeah they are bat shit crazy", and they are the ones that should be feared because in certain situations they showed no emotion, they didn't even respond. Mia would say, "I can't give my energy." Naelynne would say, "Get worked up for what? That's not my problem." My friend Christine would laugh, and say "I just stared at them." Each of them had something that I didn't have but that I wanted, restraint, and mastery over their energy. When I realized that my energy was in my control I started to apply that thought to my anger. When I walk away from something, and it follows me I have learned to be unphased and unbothered, even when my triggers are being set off. I tell myself this person, thing, spirit, demon wants my energy so can't feed it. I simply will not engage. This is not something that happens overnight it takes great restraint, and honestly I have not yet mastered it. This is a lesson that I am also teaching my son Boston, I figure if he learns it early in life it will be second nature to him.

Before learning anything about mastering or managing my own energy I would say I first took note to how I felt after leaving a reggae club. I can't dance for anything, but it is something about the music, the people, the atmosphere that will lift my spirit, and even make me want to dance. I also noticed that there were times where I felt the need to isolate myself. Most likely it would happen after being in a very crowded space such as the mall during the holidays. Normally when I return to my car I have to allow myself a moment to breathe before I start driving.

Energy is always being exchanged and unless you are mindful of it you may not even recognize it. I have worked with clients who have had soul ties, which are emotional bonds that form an attachment. The tie was so strong they needed to release themselves from it by doing actual work. Daniel and I have had energy exchanges several times throughout our relationship. We were dating and the first weekend we spent together was a great one, it was like one experience after another, the weekend went up and down, in a good way, we were learning each other, intrigued with each other, and enjoying each other. When Monday came I couldn't get out of the bed. I was so drained, despite practicing my self care Sunday routine, and resting. We did too much in one weekend, I overexerted myself in that I shared and received so much energy in the course of two days. As pleasurable as it was, I could not allow that to happen again, but it continued to happen when ever we interacted, and still does. At times we are filling each other up and other times we are draining each other. We are both passionate about certain things and this love we created is intense. I honestly don't understand it completely so I am constantly exploring it, dissecting it, and analyzing it because it is new to me. I know that I can only manage it in doses though, I have to step back, recharge, and get grounded often or it can all just explode.Be mindful of who you spend time with, and who you choose to give your time to, as it will affect your mood, views, and your ideas. Learn to protect your energy, be selfish with it.

Ever heard the saying what you put out into the universe it will come back to you 10 fold, well that includes energy as well. When you wake up with a negative mindset, you may realize the day keeps getting worse. When you decide to change your mindset, you can reset your energy to allow your day to improve. As Nipsey Hussle would say, "Learn to master your energy."

REFLECTION

In the spaces provided below, list the energy drainers in your life. Use additional paper if necessary.

Energy-Draining People

   _ 1.

   _ 2.

   _ 3.

   _ 4.

   _ 5.

Energy-Draining Emotions

 __ 1.

 __ 2.

 __ 3.

 __ 4.

 __ 5.

Energy- Drainers at work

 __ 1.

 __ 2.

 __ 3.

 __ 4.

 __ 5.

Energy- Drainers at Home

 __ 1.

 __ 2.

 __ 3.

__ *4.*

__ *5.*

Other Energy Drainers

__ *1.*

__ *2.*

__ *3.*

__ *4.*

__ *5.*

When you have completed your lists, go back and put one of the following letters in the space at the left of each number: O by the items you can overlook, and A by the items that need some action. In the space below, list some actions you can take to reduce the energy drainers marked with an A.

This excerpt is adapted from Collins, Gary. Appendix J. Christian Coaching "Helping Others Turn Potential Into Reality" 2nd Edition, Gary R. Collins. Colorado Springs, CO. 2009 (111-112) Print.

FOOD FOR THOUGHT: When you love yourself, you glow from the inside. You attract people who love, respect, and appreciate your energy. Everything starts with and how you feel about yourself. Start feeling worthy, valuable and deserving of receiving the best that life has to offer. Be magnetic.

CHAPTER 8

The 4 Ls: Live, love, learn & life

The Dalai Lama, when asked what surprised him most about humanity, answered:

"Man. Because he sacrifices his health in order to make money. Then he sacrifices money to recuperate his health. And then he is so anxious about the future that he does not enjoy the present; the result being that he does not live in the present or the future; he lives as if he is never going to die, and then dies having never really lived." Seriously, how much time are you wasting worrying about things and people you can't control. Again, you can only control yourself. I encourage you to start living and put that same energy that you spend on people, places and things that you can't control, on your self improvement and living.

Anything that annoys you is teaching you patience. Anyone who abandons you is teaching you how to stand on your own two feet. Anything that angers you is teaching you compassion. Anything that has power over you is teaching you how to take your power back. Anything you hate is teaching you unconditional love. Anything you fear is teaching you the courage to overcome your fear. Anything you can't control is teaching you how to let go and trust the Universe. All the lessons and all the things we fight and cry over are here to teach us and help us grow (Naturalabundance.blogspot.com 2011). I couldn't agree more. In the introduction of this book, I said I think everyone has a book inside of them because everyone has a story. Think about your life. Think about all the happenings; good, bad and indifferent. They all helped to shape and mold you into the person you are at this very moment. I see and hear a lot in my field. So many of my clients have so much in common. I believe that our stories are meant to be shared, not held in, but the choice is yours.

According to a study performed and written by John-Paul Iwuoha, The 5 biggest regrets people have before they die are 1) wishing they pursued their dreams/aspirations, and not the life others expect of them, 2) wished they didn't work so hard, 3) wished they had the courage to express their feelings/speak their mind, 4) wish they had stayed in touch their my friends and 5) wish they had chosen happiness. (Linkedin.com 2017). Are you living with regrets? Do you want to wait until you can't make changes to live a more fulfilling life? What will your journey be about? Start today. Choose yourself. Choose happiness. I believe in you. Do you believe in yourself? Our childhood shapes and molds us. No one is free from trials and tribulations. How one codes and deals with their experiences is what makes a difference. Although I had to grow up fast, I decided years ago that I wouldn't allow my past hardships to keep me from living a life I dreamed about living. I often sit and reflect on my journey. Traveling and culture are some of the things that sets my soul on fire and fills my tank back up. I often get questions on how I do it. I just do. Ask yourself what's holding you back. Fear? Finances? Both? Another excuse? What can you do today to make a change so you can start living the life you want to live? Take it one moment, one day at a time. One little step consistently leads to bigger changes.

I am big on manifestation and writing things down. This relates to the law of attraction, being clear on what you want, prayer, and being in a ready position, which I talked about earlier. One of the things I wanted to do in 2019 was take a solo international trip to somewhere I hadn't been before, preferably that took more than a few hours (by plane) to get to . I always wanted to visit India but didn't expect that to be the place I would visit this year. Like I always say we have to be ready when opportunities pop up and manifestation is REAL. Anywho, when the India trip became an opportunity, I was hesitant for various reasons. This included the long flight, language barriers, and the possibility of getting sick and being alone. When I sat with my concerns, I realized that even though these concerns were valid, I was letting fear rule my judgement. I switched my mindset because I am the CEO and focused on what could go right. I'm so glad I went and now I have a lifetime of memories and experiences. Courage is the ability to do something that frightens one. What do you want to do right now that you have reservations about? Live. Learn. Love. Life. Grow. Take that risk. Focus on what could go right instead of negative thoughts. The choice is yours. Will you play it safe all your life?

While I was India, the universe gave me various lessons. My favorite was on faith, patience, and trusting the process. I was so excited to see the Taj Mahal while I was visiting Agra. The morning I arrived the entire area was covered in fog and overcast. Instead of getting upset, I prayed, stayed calm, and listened to the history of this incredible wonder of the world. I then started talking to various people from all around the world and before I knew it-- not only did the sun come out; but the fog lifted! I was able to capture some amazing pictures and create lasting memories. When you truly want something and go after it without limiting disbelief, the universe will make it happen. You will never be motivated all the time, so you must learn to be disciplined. The crowd will never understand how hard you work, because they are in the stands and you are in the game.

Will you continue to play before the buzzer rings and your game is over? The choice is yours.

How often are you doing self reflection? It all starts with the person staring back at you. What areas in your life could you or should you be working on but continue putting it off? When will your tomorrow, become today? Have faith in yourself, including your gut feelings, dreams, and desires. Let down your guard, relax, and enjoy the playground of life. I know a lot of people that feel stuck, unhappy, comfortable, or even uncomfortable. If you are in that spot right now, I encourage you to dig deep. Life is too short to be anything but happy. Start taking the steps to make YOUR change. I personally have taken many risks in my lifetime. I, like you, had "fears" but I will tell you this--the Universe has its way of working things out. Never get too comfortable. Always grow and learn.

Speaking of self-reflection, at my core I am someone who genuinely cares and feels. I was always told I was too sensitive and it's something I have dealt with my entire life. I would cry too much, I would get my feelings easily hurt. I could feel other people's energy. As an adult I finally discovered that I am an empath. Being an empath is different from being empathetic. Being empathetic is when your heart goes out to someone else. Being an empath means you can actually *feel* another person's happiness or sadness in your own body. In empaths, the brain's mirror neuron system – a specialized group of cells that are responsible for compassion- is thought to be hyperactive. As a result, empaths can absorb other people's energies both positive and negative into their own bodies. At times it may even be difficult to tell if you're feeling your own emotions or someone else's (Judith 2019). According to (Judith 2019), Empaths are the medicine the world needs and they can have a profound impact on humanity with their compassion and understanding.

I care about people. I care about matters. Like how people are feeling, how I can possibly help, etc. I like helping whether it's being a sounding board or physically volunteering. I have observed that caring and giving sometimes leaves you feeling some type of way—not always good. This "not good" can turn into negative energy and can often times make one turn into someone or something they're not. (I.E. Treat people the way they were treated) For me, it becomes a bit difficult when I have to try and be someone that I am not. I am only good at being me. However, I will say that I have reached a point of maturity and growth in which I had to step back and reevaluate this energy exchange. I often sit with myself and process many questions, thoughts, and feelings. What I have come up with so far: People don't necessarily treat you how you treat them and that's okay, even though it may hurt or sting at times. I can only be responsible for my actions, my words, my work, my mistakes, and my growth. Some people are fighting internal battles that I know nothing about and these battles appear in different forms. Moreover, the complexity and depth of my concepts have inspired me to continue to be me; while still learning how to find a balance between giving and protecting my energy. I have learned and I am still learning how to not take things personally. However, I recognize that along my journey disappointment and obstacles may arise and that is okay too as we all have our own passage of development and growth. I hope this inspires someone to 1) do their work 2) not take things personally 3) keep on keeping on.

"Even when it's not pretty or perfect. Even when it's more real than you want it to be. Your story is what you have, and what you will always have. It is something to own." (Obama, 2018)

LIVE LOVE LEARN LIFE this is my motto in life Live life with no regrets, in abundance, and without fear of failure. Live without limits, and live intentionally.

There is not one thing in this life that I regret, not one word, one action, one decision or one thought, for they have shaped me, taught me, and showed me something about myself and my life. I try to live in abundance because life is honestly too short not to soak in its joy, or waste it on the dissatisfaction of minute things. If you live in fear that means you are putting the saying forget everything and run to practice, when you live without fear that means you are willing to face everything and rise. To live without limits means to not allow anyone, yourself included to put you in a box, and limit you to what their idea of you is instead of what your heart and mind tells you you are. To live intentionally means to figure out your purpose in life, and pursue it with everything you have in you.

Love, love is exhausting but it is worth it. Yes that is coming from me, the woman who has gone through two divorces, saying love is worth it. Love the experience, the process, and fall in love with the journey. Love the people in your life, love people as they are, and love your enemies, and most importantly love yourself. When you need to be reminded of what love is remember 1 Corinthians 13:4–8a"Love is patient and kind. Love is not jealous or boastful or proud or rude. It does not demand its own way. It is not irritable, and it keeps no record of being wronged. It does not rejoice about injustice but rejoices whenever the truth wins out. Love never gives up, never loses faith, is always hopeful, and endures through every circumstance ... love will last forever!"

Learn, you will continue to go through it until you learn the lesson. Learn to appreciate it, learn to "forgive yourself for not knowing what you didn't know until you lived through it. Learn to honor your path. Trust your journey. Learn, grow, evolve, become." -Creig Crippen

Life, is precious, its beautiful, and it's real. "Life is growth, if we stop growing, technically and spiritually, we are as good as dead". -Moriher Ueshiba Have you ever considered what it takes to give something life? Be it a flower, a vegetable, a person or idea. It all starts with a seed that is nurtured and grown until it evolves into what it was meant to be. Every day we are given a new opportunity at life, and it is simply what we make it. There is no right or wrong way to live as we are all on this journey, at different stages, and trying to figure it out as we go along. You are exactly where you are suppose to be, stop right now comparing yourself to someone else, stop judging yourself using someone else's standards, start to appreciate your life and who you are in this world.

FOOD FOR THOUGHT: There is a time to be born and a time to die. What are you doing in between these times? Embrace uncertainty. Some of the most beautiful chapters in our lives won't have a title until much later. Stop existing and start living!

CHAPTER 9

Invest in yourself & get out of your own way

Your time as a caterpillar has expired. Your wings are ready for you to fly. I remember reading Tyrese's "How to Get Out of Your Own Way," years ago. I really didn't know what he meant before reading the book but as I started reading the book, it started to make so much sense to me. Basically, we self-sabotage ourselves in life. We overthink. We over analyze. We talk ourselves out of taking the steps to reach our goals. We compare ourselves to others. We want what others have (Gibson 2012). Stay true to YOUR vision, goals, and plans. They were placed inside you for a reason. Start now. Start where you are. Start with "fear". Start with pain. Start with doubt. Start with anxiety. Start with depression. Start with what you have. Start and don't stop. You can do it! In life, we have choices--pointing out again, the only thing we can control is ourselves. How you react, how you grow, and ultimately how you choose to live. In the midst of chaos, I encourage you to choose peace. In the midst of sadness, I encourage you to choose happiness. The choice is yours.

The one person I am always willing to bet on is myself. That means I will take a chance on love, my dreams, my businesses, and my choices. What is the worst that can happen? Mistakes, hurt, betrayal are all apart of learning. The flip side of this is that beautiful things can happen and be discovered. One of my favorite online mentors and life coaches, Tony Gaskins, sent out an email a while back that had some great food for thought in it: What about you? What is it you want? What do you need to do? When is the last time you had a massage? When is the last time you went on a walk alone? When is the last time you treated yourself to a date with yourself? Do you know what your heart wants and needs in this season of your life? If not, it's time to fall deeper in love with you and your dreams. Because we are humans, we all need these moments to self-reflect and reset our mind, body, and soul. If you don't go after what you want, you will never have it. If you don't ask, the answer will always be no. If you don't step forward you will always be in the same place. Are you tired of having the same issues in your life? You have the power and choice to make a change whether it's with your finances, with love, or with toxic exchanges.

The universe has a way of making things work out in your favor when you put out positive energy and speak things into existence. For instance, If you are trying to buy a home, get a promotion at work, wanting to start your business, or waiting on that special someone -- speak and claim it into existence. Start manifesting your blessings. Here's some examples: Thank you in advance Lord for my financial freedom. Thank you Lord for my blooming business. Thank you Lord for my amazing partner. I encourage you to start right now. What blessings are you going to manifest in your life? You think you aren't good enough, but you are. You think you can't do it, but you can. You think it's too late, but it's not. The secret to getting ahead is getting started. A dream written down with a date becomes a goal. A goal broken down becomes a plan. A plan backed by action becomes reality.

My ongoing work has been not to take things personally, being comfortable in the unknown and no matter how much I plan, things will not always turn out the way I want or expect. The only thing I can control is how I show up and react to these happenings. I also have been working on living in a gray area. This means for most of my life I was white and black. It had to be one way or the other. Sometimes life doesn't work like that and you have to stay in the gray area until it's time to cross over to a side. I am slowly learning to be comfortable with the unknown as unsettling as it can be, I have days where I am at peace with it and others where I'm anxious to see what the future holds. Another area where I have had to constantly work on is my frustration when it comes to people questioning my motives. Having the heart I have is challenging. I give and help so much because I know what it is to be without. This can sometimes be taken as fake or as if I am doing it to expect something in return. Sometimes people will take advantage of this so it's important to find balance. I have definitely had my share of lessons in this area.Maybe your story is you were abandoned or you never knew your parents. Maybe you were robbed of your childhood. Maybe you were adopted. Maybe you were touched. Maybe you did time. Maybe you have/had an addiction. Maybe you never felt heard or good enough. Maybe you are struggling with your identity. Whatever you story is know that you are here for a reason. You are unique and special. You are super. You need to ignore what everyone else is doing and achieving. Your life is about breaking your own limits and outgrowing yourself to live your best life. You are not in competition with anyone else. Plan to outdo your past, not other people. I am wishing the best to anyone struggling right now. May you find the relief you desire and the resolution you need. Keep going, you got this.

"The true way to improve yourself to be the best version of you and serve those around you is by investing in yourself" - Roy T. Bennett

My question is, how can you expect someone to take a chance on you when you won't even take a chance on yourself? The simple act of purchasing this book was an investment in yourself. If you completed the reflections in this book then you invested in yourself. You invested in starting the process of doing your work, learning yourself even more deeply, and being honest with yourself.

Every day we go to work, from 9-5 or whatever shift is given to us, and help someone who has taken a chance on themselves grow their company and line their pockets. Now I know, not everyone was meant to be or even has the desire to be a business owner, or entrepreneur. I know most of us are just grateful we have income, and there is nothing wrong with that, but this still applies to you. Have you ever wondered what would happen if you were to lose your job, what if they decided to replace you? How would you start again? If you don't know the answer to this question then you should invest in yourself further. Did you hear about the sisters who started their cheesecake business to make extra money during the government shutdown? Just this past year the government shut down leaving them without pay. They each have husbands who can not work due to disabilities, bills and college tuitions to pay, and they said, "They had to do something." The thing is your knowledge as well as the skills you have developed will remain with you regardless of the economy and you can use that as a bartering tool for your next job. When you are going to work every day, the most important investment should still be you. What can this company offer you to advance and grow? I have been with my current company for 7 years. Some might think well I thought you had your own practice. I do have my own practice, but my full time job has allotted me the time I need to run my business, maintain my family, and invest further in myself. They have a great benefits package, and I was able to get reimbursed for earning my masters degree. I stay up to date on my continuing education credits as it allows me to remain marketable, employable, and competitive. Networking is a great way to invest in yourself and promote growth socially, and build confidence in your brand which is essentially YOU regardless if you are a business owner, entrepreneur, or a store clerk, you are your own brand. Networking allows you to meet new people, share ideas, and become inspired.

Investing in yourself doesn't have to be monetary either it could also mean practicing self care, eating right, exercising regularly, and seeking therapy. Regardless if you are a college student, a mother of five, an entrepreneur, or just on this journey YOU are the most important part of your YOUniverse, you are the most important source of your wealth.

<u>REFLECTION</u>

What are your strengths, what do you do well?

_____

_____

_____

What are your weaknesses?

_____

_____

_____

In what ways do you limit yourself?

_____

_____

_____

Review your previous answers and list the ways can you invest in yourself today?

_____

_____

_____

FOOD FOR THOUGHT: When will you stop hitting the snooze button on your life? When will you start living?If you have time to feel bad, complain and check social media then you have time to meditate, write in your journal, create a list of goals, make a list of things you are grateful for and better yourself.

CHAPTER 10

Knowing your worth

D on't mistake my positivity for a lack of struggle. I am a sinner, been broken, and did not know my worth and God still rescued me. Do you know who you are? What you like and don't like? It seems like a trivial question but so many people are not able to answer this question. I will admit it has taken me years to figure out who I am and it is still a process. Once you figure out your worth, you will stop giving people discounts. Forgive yourself for everything you allowed before you knew your worth. Forgive yourself for allowing people to mistreat you, disrespect you, or use you. Forgive yourself for not not knowing better at the time. Forgive yourself for giving away your power. Forgive yourself for past behaviors. Forgive yourself for the survival patterns and traits you picked up while enduring trauma. Forgive yourself for being who you needed to be. You are now better for it and needed those lessons in order to be where you are today. Be alone. Eat alone. Take yourself on dates. In the midst of this, you will learn about yourself. You will grow, you will figure out what inspires you. You will curate your dreams, beliefs, and gain a general clarity of self. When various people come into your life and different circumstances come up you can act from a place of certainty because you are sure of yourself.Who am I? I am the first born child of my parents union. I was born in Queens, New York but raised in New Jersey. As a child I loved playing outside, but was known as a tattletale when it came to kid drama. I was often called bossy. I used to love playing with dolls, playing dress up, and playing school. I also had a tomboy phase were riding bikes and playing with the boys was my thing. We played video games and various outdoor games. I remember my Dad having to call for me to come in when the street lights came on. I was always a leader and wanted people to do the right thing. It was not always easy doing the "right" thing but I never had a hard time with peer pressure. Remember the dichotomy part about my identity? I was arrested at seventeen for a shoplifting stunt at a local mall. I had the money to pay for those earrings but I got a high and an escape from the current situation I was in then (motel living). This incident resulted in several fines and classes. That was a lesson I learned and never had a brush with the law again.

I have loved, broke some hearts, and had my heart broken. I have lied and been lied to. I have been that gossipy mean girl. I was teased as a kid. Kids can be cruel and I still remember kids singing the 1-800-99-Jenny commercial when I was in elementary school. Although I have been up and down weight

113

wise in life, back then it was more related to my first and last name Jennifer Gregg rhyming with the song from Jenny Craig than the actual advertisement of weight loss. I am a hopeless romantic and love serendipity. I love going out but enjoy staying in and believe your home should be a safe place to recharge. I believe in promises and keeping my word. I am a dreamer and a doer. I am highly intuitive and energy is my first language. I am type A and super organized to my own detriment at times. I am love in action and lean towards leading with my heart is most situations. I love celebrating birthdays. I love throwing parties and hosting events. I enjoy cooking and sharing my cooking with others. I am a hobby baker. I absolutely love traveling, meeting new people, and sharing life stories. I am a hard worker but believe in work/life balance. I love shopping for clothes but do not like food shopping and doing laundry. I am a daughter, sister, lover, friend, cousin, God Mom and a successful serial entrepreneur. I am a coach. I am a humanitarian. I am a life learner. I want to inspire and heal people. I am a masterpiece and a work in progress. I am constantly growing, learning, and evolving all while remembering to live and love.

Real growth starts when you start checking and correcting yourself. You can't always be right because that would mean you are perfect and never make mistakes. I was not always the person I am today. I have been the mean girl, the toxic person in various people's lives. I have said some hurtful mean things. I have called people names, talked about people behind their back and they found out. For that, I publicly apologize. I have tried reaching out to the people I have caused hurt to and apologized. Remember when I said healing the inner child is so important? This unhealing can come out in ways like this. Being nasty, petty, gossiping, and hurting others. Until you address this inner child these negative behaviors will continue to render their ugly heads. Getting back to the people I have apologized to for my behavior, some were receptive and others were not. That is and was their choice just like my choice was to apologize. I can only control and have responsibility over myself and my own actions. I have also had to accept apologies that I know I was owed, that to date I have not received. If the universe sees it fit for me to receive these, I will. If not, I am at peace with every matter that has transpired to date. They all happened for a reason. They all are a part of my story, and I made the choice to not stay in that chapter. I am grateful for the lessons in all these experiences.

One of the last gifts my Dad gave me before he passed was a little candle holder that has on it *"Jennifer, your confidence shows in all you do."* Months after his passing, we moved into a development that unbeknownst to us would need mandatory fire sprinkler repair work. The association required all residents to be uprooted and placed in a temporary apartment for six weeks. Before we moved out, we were asked to put away all personal items and cover everything else with sheets or the equivalent to prevent dust and debris from getting on the furniture, etc. Six weeks passed, and we move back into our place. I will admit I do have a slight case of OCD and right away noticed my candle holder was MIA. I looked, looked, and looked and couldn't find it anywhere. I called up the association to explain that my candle holder was MIA and how it was one of the last things my deceased Father gave to me. The lady I spoke to probably thought I was insane, but I insisted that she ask every single worker that was in my house if they had seen it. She did and one of the workers admitted to dropping the candle holder and throwing it away. I insisted that the worker go find where he threw it out and get me the pieces. He did, and I glued them back together. Takeaway: Be your own advocate, don't be so quick to take "no" as a final answer, things get shattered all the time but there are options to "fix" them, and Life happens to everyone.

Sarah Jakes wrote a blog on the Beauty of the unknown. There will come a moment when all that matters to you is that you experience growth, not comfort. When that time comes it will shake your world up. It will cause you to expand into areas of thought that you never thought possible. It will be liberating and isolating. It takes a special kind of person to resist comfort and to press into the unknown. The unknown is scary. It reveals your vulnerabilities and insecurities. The unknown is where you discover the layers of who you were created to be. If we are not careful we will see the unknown as a place where all we can do is survive. The survival mentality does not allow for you to glean the lessons this season is committed to teaching you. I'm not sure what your unknown is. Perhaps you've just gotten a new job. Maybe you're dealing with something in your relationship. For some of you, this may be the first time you've ever been alone. Don't allow the uncertainty to make you shut down. If you attempt to build walls when God is trying to tear your walls down you will end up stuck (Sarah Jakes Roberts 2019). What dead weight such as people, places, and things are you holding onto that you need to get rid of? Cutting out the "dead" makes room for new growth and lightens your load. My favorite season is Fall better known as the beautiful Autumn. Not just because of the fashion and temperature but because Autumn shows us how beautiful it is to let things go.

So what? You dated a person, fell for them and they broke your heart into a million pieces and you learned a hard lesson. You chose the wrong major and had to start again. You cherished a friend who turned their back on you. Your family member borrowed money and went MIA. Your family member called you something you know you're not. Your family member stabbed you in the back. Someone you trusted broke their promise. It's life. We learn, hurt, love, cry, laugh, trust and do it all over again. Experiences make you unique. Embrace your uniqueness. Your outlook will determine your outcome. It is okay to make mistakes, to have bad days, to be less than "perfect" (because what and who is really perfect?), to do what's best for you, and to just be yourself. Just because the past didn't turn out like you wanted it to, doesn't mean your future can't be better than you have ever imagined.

I mentioned in the beginning of the book, part of doing my work was to do my research on my parents and how they got to where they did financially. I used to have so much resentment and was closed-minded. I didn't understand how two college educated people that came from well-to-do families could make poor decisions that left us in the financial predicament and issues we faced. I didn't understand a lot before I made the choice to start doing my work. I also mentioned that there are three sides to every story. I don't know all three sides but I do know that I can't judge how my parents showed up in this lifetime. In general, I believe that they both didn't get a chance to address and heal their inner child. They both had major losses at such young ages and they eventually attracted each other. Trauma, hurt and other life happenings show up differently for everyone. Sometimes it will not make sense just because it's something you may or may not do. Sometimes it's not for us to understand. Law of attraction is real as I have said before. Everyone deals with life differently and I think my parents did the best they could with the tools they had. They made various choices that lead us in the various situations we experienced, I have made the choice to view my past in a way that helps fuel my future. I would not be who I am today without my parents, two of my most important journey teachers.

I often advise clients to have compassion for themselves. Be softer with yourself and remember that you are a breathing thing. You are human. You are a memory to someone and a home to a life. According to Buddha, what you think you become. What you feel, you attract. What you imagine, you create. In Japan, broken objects are often repaired with Gold. The flaw is seen as a unique piece of the object's history, which adds to its beauty. Consider this when you feel broken.

As we come to a close, I have all the feels. Writing this book really took me down memory lane. It brought up emotions and feelings that I had forgotten about. Thank you for taking the journey with me. Thank you for your time and energy. Thank you for investing in yourself. I am wishing you so much love, peace, and light with wherever you are at this very moment. If you remember nothing else I said, please remember the choice is yours and if no one else believes in you, I do. Please, please, please live while you're here.

Xo, Coach J

***"Our deepest fear is not that we are inadequate, our greatest fear is that we are powerful beyond measure"* - Marianne Williamson**

Oh baby when I say there is something that happens when you realize just who you are. When you realize that you are uniquely made, and there is only one you. Your quirks, your personality, your thoughts, even the "ugly you" makes you just who you are.

My first business was named VIP Weddings and Events. I loved planning events, but what I didn't love was networking or even promoting my business. I didn't want to be the face of my company. When I first started out, I was self-conscious about my blackness offending someone. I thought that if they knew I was black they would not want to work with me. I mean it was to the point I had a white coworker leave my voice mail greeting for my business phone. I was not always like that; it wasn't until my first marriage. My first husband was white. In that relationship, I learned firsthand that people were still racist, it blew my mind. Up until then I never thought about being black, or about being anything other than Courtney. But I quickly learned just how black I was. It didn't matter the degrees I held, it didn't matter my upbringing, some people only saw color and judged you based off it. When I would go to class, I started to notice things such as there was only one other black person in there. When I was completing my internship, I went to a meeting and something felt strange. I couldn't pinpoint it, and then it came to me, I was the only black person in the room, and I was a woman. What triggered this was the stories my husband at the time would come home with, stories about how his boss hated black people. During that time the election was going on, circa 2007-2008 when Obama ran for office for the first time eventually to serve during his first term. He would tell me that his boss would say things, such as, "If I hear that any of you voted for that monkey, I am firing them on the spot." One day in particular he came home from work upset, and shared that a coworker made a statement about Christina Aguilera being contaminated. I said, "Oh no what happened to her, how did she get contaminated?" I was genuinely concerned, he went on to say, his coworker made that statement because she was sleeping with a black man. I would say that was my wake-up call. Today I am so pro black, oh and proud. I care about helping others, but my main focus is on the advancement of my people. If my blackness offends you, that is your problem. If my hair offends you, that is your problem. If the natural tone in my voice offends you, then again that is your problem. Remember I told you I value every relationship I have had. My first marriage showed me certain things about people (they are not all good), some are judging you based off their ignorance, and it is not for me to change their perception or convince them of anything different. If my blackness offends you then I am not for you, neither is my business. I will no longer hide, I will not conform, because I am black first. If you look at my current logo it is of a black woman floating with a huge afro, (ascension). I know my worth. My skin is made from the same elements of the universe, my hair defies gravity, my smile lights up a room, and my eyes are so big and beautiful you can lose yourself in them. Outside of my looks, I am smart, I am courageous, I am kind, I am powerful, I have the gift of vision, and insight. I am a goddess in my own right. I can manifest and bring the things I want to fruition. I multiply anything I touch; I add value to the things I am involved with. I am multifaceted, well rounded, and so down to earth that I can fit in anywhere. Again, we are all living this life and it is the experiences, and how we respond to them that shape us. My worth is not determined by anything material, or anything tangible, it is not based off my hair or my looks. My worth is the value I see in myself. Because I know my worth, I set the tone for how others treat me. I set the narrative. There are people who won't even consider buying this book because they have made up in their minds, they already know who I am, how I think, or where I belong. I make a lot of people uncomfortable because I am constantly growing and evolving. I am no longer that little girl who would pop you in the mouth if you popped off, I have grown into a woman who can assess who and what needs my attention. I was a tomboy, I was a little rough around the edges, and some people can't get out of their heads who they use to know, or who my parents were. So, when I stand before them today, in my audacity to be who I am and not what they thought I would amount to, they are either in awe or utterly disturbed. My aunt on my father's side said, "Courtney girl I am so proud of you, you really turned out to be a beautiful person, you don't look anything like what you have been through".

Knowing your worth comes from how you value yourself. It is not based on what others think of you, what you have or have not accomplished, it is how you feel on the inside. The likes and following mean nothing when it comes to your self-worth. I want to end by saying the choice is yours, this life is yours. All you must do is decide what you want, and how you want to live. You don't have to settle for anything in this life, you are worthy of all that you desire.

I wish you love and light on your journey

Courtney Gardner

REFLECTIONS

I AM STATEMENTS (USE THE SPACE BELOW TO WRITE I AM STATEMENTS) don't hold back, this is not the time to be humble write down all of what you are. BRAG!

I Am_____

I Am_____

I Am_____

I Am_____

I Am_____

I Am_____

I Am_____

I Am_____

I Am_____

I Am_____

*FOOD FOR THOUGHT: Everyone has their own journey. We all come from different backgrounds and therefore have different paths to success. Success looks and feels different for everyone. Happiness is a journey not a destination. The Choice is ultimately yours.

BONUS

Here is some food for thought followed by a journal prompt. It is our hope these jewels can be used throughout your journey.

- Be open to universal blessings. Remember sometimes these come in the form of lessons.

- Enjoy the mystery and beauty of life.

- Embrace change.

- When things don't turn out exactly how we wanted, planned, or expected trust that everything happens for a reason and adjust accordingly.

- When you apologize for something be sincere, say I apologize versus I'm sorry...words are powerful...think about it.

- Be careful and clear about what you pray and wish for.

- There is room for everyone to win.

- Some people will want to see you do good but not better than them. That's their problem, not yours.

- If you can help someone, do so.

- There is compensation on the other side of service.

- You can't change the past .

- Not everyone will see and understand your heart and light. Light attracts moths, too.

- You were enough yesterday, You are enough today, and you will be enough tomorrow.

- The Choice is Yours

If you have ever had a diary, you know that it is meant to collect your thoughts of your day. You may write down your experiences, your feelings, and more. But typically, you would always write down what happened, not what will happen or what you want to happen. Today we are urging you to keep a different type of journal, one where you diligently write down what you want to happen and what your dreams will bring to your life in terms of happiness and success. Even though it may not happen that way exactly, it is a good way to program yourself for success. I always say your words, thoughts, and vision have power and there is power in the penPlease use this space below to start speaking your life into existence.

AFFIRM: My life is about to change drastically. All that I have been working on and visualizing is about to manifest for me. All my effort and dedication is about to pay off in a major way. I am so grateful and I feel so blessed to know that everything is happening for me.

_____

Courtney Gardner & Jennifer Gregg

Meet the Authors:

**Courtney Gardner, Success Coach, CSW,
M.A. in Human Service Counseling,
Author, Owner, & Success Coach of
The Art of Ascending LLC**

With a passion for helping others, Courtney started her career as a mentor for at-risk youth. She earned her undergraduate degree from Rutgers University where she then went on to become a Social Worker who advocates for, links, and stabilizes, developmentally disabled individuals, children, and families in the mental & behavioral health community. Courtney decided to further her education and obtained her Masters in Human Service Counseling with a minor in Life Coaching from

Liberty University. With over ten years of experience in the field, Courtney has a natural gift to motivate those around her. In 2016 she founded The Art of Ascending LLC a professional life coaching practice where she works with motivated individuals providing guidance to her clients who crave progression and Ascension. Stay in touch with Courtney at www.theartofascending.com

Jennifer Gregg, B.A., M.S. is a certified life coach, author, and the founder of J. Gregg's Journey Innovations, LLC (JGJI). Through her modern-day coaching business, Jennifer a.k.a. Coach Jen, provides both in-person and virtual sessions for individuals and groups, as well as life skills training, corporate team building workshops, along with empowerment and motivational talks for youth and adults.

Coach Jen's educational background in Psychology and Sociology, coupled with her advanced degree in Behavioral Studies has prepared her to offer practical guidance in the areas of grief support, stress management, goal setting, and life organizing. Coach Jen also has over a decade's worth of experience offering emotional support to children and is a former social worker with the NJ Department of Child Protection and Permanency. Beyond her authoritative qualifications, Coach Jen's own story of overcoming childhood trauma and rebuilding after a parental loss, gives her a unique perspective on what it takes to heal, organize, and thrive.

While everyone has their own journey, Coach Jen believes that great energy, self-disclosure, being clear, staying organized and following through, creates a level of trust and comfort that ultimately helps foster a great client and coach relationship. To get started on your journey with Coach Jen email Coach@jgreggji.com to schedule your consultation today.

A Life Coach is a professional who helps you reach a goal or make a change in your life. They help you to get out of your own way and start acting in the areas of your life that you wish to change. They also play the important roles of motivator, strategist, and accountability partner. Life Coaches help clients reach his/her goal(s) in the most efficient, effective and rewarding way possible. They are more than just a counselor or consultant, they step you through the achievement process from the beginning to the end, from the planning stage all the way through the execution stages. Studies have been done on how effective life coaching is and some are based on ROI, some are based on the satisfaction of the client and their willingness to return. Both types of studies have proven the effectiveness of life coaching.

*Areas that life coaches handle:

*Work-life balance

*Health and fitness

*Spirituality

*Work performance

*Career goals

*Procrastination & productivity

*Getting motivated

*Finding your purpose

*Prioritization

*Hobbies

*Educational goals

*Dating and sex

*Divorce

*ADHD

*Organization

Visit www.jgreggji.com for more information and keeping in touch with Coach Jennifer.

References

Buckingham, W. (2012). *Happiness: A Practical Guide*. London: Icon.

Burley-Allen, M. (1995). *Listening: the forgotten skill*. New York: John Wiley & Sons.

Collins, G. R. (2014). *Christian coaching helping others turn potential into reality*. United States: The Navigators.

Gibson, T. and Tyrese (2012). *How to get out of your own way*. New York: Grand Central Pub.

Judith, O. (2019). *Are You an Empath? Take this 20 Question Empath Test - Judith Orloff MD*. [online] Judith Orloff MD. Available at: https://drjudithorloff.com/quizzes/empath-self-assessment-test/ [Accessed 11 Sep. 2019].

Linkedin.com. (2017). *This Study Reveals The 5 Biggest Regrets People Have Before They Die*. [online] Available at: https://www.linkedin.com/pulse/study-reveals-5-biggest-regrets-people-have-before-die-iwuoha/ [Accessed 21 Aug. 2019].

Manson, M. (2016). *The Subtle Art of Not Giving a Fuck A Counterintuitive Approach to Living a Good Life.* New York: HarperOne.

Naturalabundance.blogspot.com. (2011). *Poems and Quotes*. [online] Available at:

http://naturalabundance.blogspot.com/p/poems-and-quotes.html [Accessed 13 June. 2017].

Neustaeter, Brooklyn. (2016, June 16). 10 Things that Hold More Importance in a Relationship than Love. Retrieved from http://www.narcity.com/ [Accessed 15 September. 2019].

Nimh.nih.gov. (2019). *NIMH » Depression.* [online] Available at: https://www.nimh.nih.gov/health/topics/depression/index.shtml [Accessed 29 Aug. 2019].

Obama, M. (2018). *Becoming.* New York: Crown.

Petersen, J. C. (2007). *Why Don't We Listen Better?: Communicating & Connecting in Relationships.* Portland, OR: Petersen.

ProFlowers Blog. (2019). *History and Meaning of Sunflowers - ProFlowers Blog.* [online] Available at: https://www.proflowers.com/blog/history-and-meaning-of-sunflowers [Accessed 19 Sep. 2019].

Sarah Jakes Roberts. (2019). *The Beauty in the Unknown — Sarah Jakes Roberts.* [online] Available at: https://sarahjakesroberts.com/blog/2017/9/19/the-beauty-in-the-unknown [Accessed 29 Aug. 2019].

Stewart, J. R. (2012). *Bridges not walls: a book about interpersonal communication.* New York: McGraw-Hill.

Thích-thiênh-Tâm . (1994). *Buddhism of wisdom and faith.* Northern Hills , CA : Horizontal Escape.

Thomas, K. W. (2007). *Calling in "The One": 7 Weeks to Attract the Love of Your Life.* New York, NY: Harmony.

www.ingramcontent.com/pod-product-compliance
Lightning Source LLC
Chambersburg PA
CBHW021236090426
42740CB00006B/562